ON METHOD

▲ ▲ ▲ ▲ ▲ ▲ ▲ ▲ ▲ ▲ ▲ ▲ ▲ ▲ ▲ ▲ ▲ ▲ ▲

By DAVID BAKAN

ON METHOD

THE DUALITY OF HUMAN EXISTENCE

SIGMUND FREUD AND THE
JEWISH MYSTICAL TRADITION

DISEASE, PAIN, AND SACRIFICE
(*In press*)

DAVID BAKAN

♣ ♣ ♣ ♣ ♣ ♣ ♣ ♣ ♣ ♣ ♣ ♣ ♣ ♣ ♣ ♣ ♣ ♣ ♣ ♣

ON METHOD

★ ★ ★ ★ ★ ★ ★ ★ ★ ★ ★ ★ ★ ★ ★ ★ ★ ★ ★

Toward a Reconstruction
of Psychological
Investigation

Jossey-Bass Inc., Publishers
615 Montgomery Street · San Francisco · 1967

ON METHOD: TOWARD A RECONSTRUCTION
OF PSYCHOLOGICAL INVESTIGATION
   by David Bakan

Copyright © 1967 by Jossey-Bass, Inc., Publishers

Copyright under Pan American and
Universal Copyright Conventions

Jossey-Bass, Inc., Publishers
615 Montgomery Street
San Francisco, California 94111

Library of Congress Catalog Card Number 67–28628

Printed in the United States of America
by York Composition Company, Inc.
York, Pennsylvania

FIRST EDITION

6798

THE JOSSEY-BASS BEHAVIORAL SCIENCE SERIES

General Editors
WILLIAM E. HENRY, *University of Chicago*
NEVITT SANFORD, *Stanford University*

Preface

To name this collection of essays, I have borrowed the term "reconstruction" from John Dewey's little book *Reconstruction in Philosophy* (1950). In that book Dewey discussed the way in which the opening of the human mind in modern scientific exploration was associated with the general enlargement of human interactions from the sixteenth and seventeenth centuries onward. "The mind became used to exploration and discovery. It found delight and interest in the revelations of the novel and the unusual, while it no longer took in what was old and customary. Moreover, the very act of exploration, of expedition, the process of enterprising adventure into the remote, yielded a peculiar joy and thrill" (p. 54). I don't quite see that we, as psychologists, are producing much knowledge to thus delight and thrill. Quite the contrary.

I believe that there is a crisis in research in psychology. Though enormous resources are being expended for psychological research, the yield of new and significant information concerning the nature of the human psyche is relatively small in comparison. We may appreciate why this should be the case by considering the garden variety of experiment "run" by students aspiring to win higher degrees, not to mention the experiments of many of their professors. It characteristically involves converting observational data to numbers, calculating statistics on these numbers, and applying tests of significance to these statistics. The fact of the matter is that this kind of experimentation, with the abrogations that generally go along with it—characteristically in the very name of science—cannot yield much information, and certainly little that is particularly novel. And, as many can attest, "running" an experiment in this manner is hardly an exercise conducive to overcoming mental inertia and sluggishness as science should do. I am not addressing myself to the laboriousness of the procedures. There was adventure even in the arduousness of the early studies involving lifting weights, memorizing nonsense syllables, presenting dogs with musical tones and meat powder, and listening to neurotics literally for hours on end. Nor, clearly, am I arguing against the experimental method as such.

Brentano (1874), at the time of the founding of modern experimental psychology, argued that psychology should be empirical rather than experimental; that the experiment was too far removed from experience to be able to tell us much that was significant. The very distinction—let alone the comparison—between the empirical and the experimental is one which many psychologists today might find hard to understand. In the culture of contemporary psychology the words are used synonymously. It is perhaps worthwhile to allow the possibility that the experimental may *sometimes* stand in the way of the empirical. The essential feature of any empirical epistemology is that it relies heavily on the contributions from experience. If the experimental method as it has developed in the field of psychology interferes with the processes whereby we may acquire knowledge from experience, then indeed do we have to review seriously the relationships between the experimental and the empirical.

Most experimentation in the field of psychology falls considerably short of being able to be considered really empirical. Consider the ideal of the "well-designed experiment." The usual meaning of "well-designed" is that the outcomes of the experiment have been completely anticipated, and that one will not allow the experience of conducting the experiment to lead one to consider alternatives outside of the ones already thought of beforehand.

Some years ago I developed a lecture of advice to graduate students on the conduct of research. My intent was hardly cynical. Yet this lecture was consistently interpreted by my students as cynical, a reaction that helped me to understand the very poor state of psychological research. The major point of the lecture, repeatedly made in various presentations of "good experimental design," was that the manner in which the data were to be analyzed and interpreted should be thought out carefully before the data were collected. Ideally, I argued, one should be able to write up the sections defining the problem, reviewing the literature, and explaining the methods used, exactly as they would appear in the final report. One could then proceed to block out the tables that one would report, and to write two or three different versions of the discussion section—without collecting any data whatsoever! Indeed, I argued, it was a good exercise to fill in the tables with some "made up" data to make sure that the data one eventually collected could be used to defend the assertions one would eventually make. If an experiment were thus carefully "designed," in effect, the ultimate report of the research could be simply the report written beforehand, with a few minor changes based on the data actually collected. In the context of the culture of contemporary psychological research this is very good advice. However, it must also be true that a research enterprise conducted on the basis of such advice simply cannot be considered to be predominantly empirical, for the experience of confronting phenomena, to learn what they have to teach, including deviations from expectation, plays a relatively small role in this kind of research enterprise.

Some of the experts in the modern craft of getting grants to conduct research have operated on the principle of being "one ahead." To be "one ahead" means to apply for a grant for a piece of research that one has already conducted, and to use the money thus obtained to conduct further research. When one thus works "one ahead" it is possible to write rather splendid applications. Cynical as this approach may appear, it is actually sounder from a scientific point of view than conducting research based on so-called good design. For the fact of the matter is that good research into the unknown cannot be well designed, in the usual sense of the term. Truly good research means that one allows the investigation to be guided by the experiences of the investigation. And this cannot be predicted. If it can be predicted, then there is little information to be obtained from the research; and considerably less reason to do the research. The complex theory of information based on the work of Shannon (Shannon and Weaver, 1949) rests on the very sensible observation that an information gain is the difference between initial and final ignorance. The experiment that is well designed, in the usual sense, is equally well designed to keep this difference small.

The chapter I have placed first in this book deals with the test of significance, that methodological keystone of the majority of studies in contemporary psychology. As will be seen, the test of significance is such that it yields little or no information in most of the instances in which it is used in psychological research. One has a right to ask of a science that it should satisfy some minimal criteria of empiricality and rationality. As will become evident, the test of significance in the context of its application stands in the way of both.

However, addiction to the test of significance is only a symptom indicative of a deeper disorder in contemporary psychology, a scientism which stands in the way of psychology being scientific. The propositions of a science should apply to the subject matter that the science presumes to deal with. They should have a high likelihood of being true. The research enterprise should be self-corrective. Findings should be reliable. There should be a systematic place in the research enterprise for the thought and experience of the investigator. The science should not presuppose what it is yet to discover. These would be some of the criteria that a science should fulfil. If psychology were less scientistic it could become more scientific.

The chapters in this book were written over a period of years and for various occasions. The sequence in which they have been arranged represents only a judgment of small conviction of a way by which they may be usefully read consecutively. I would hope that no reader will be bound by that judgment. Roughly, critical papers are first and then efforts at other possible ways of pursuing and thinking about the psychological enterprise. I have much more conviction in the critical remarks I have made than in the other possibilities. My aim has been more to open possibilities than to advocate them, even though the temptation to do the latter is always great.

Chicago, Illinois   *David Bakan*

Contents

xvii

Contents

ON METHOD

♣ 1

The Test of Significance
in
Psychological Research

The vast majority of investigations which pass for research in the field of psychology today entail the use of statistical tests of significance. Most characteristically, when a psychologist finds a problem he wishes to investigate he converts his intuitions and hypotheses into procedures which will yield a test of significance, and will characteristically allow the result of the test of significance to bear the essential responsibility for the conclusions he will draw.

I will attempt to show that the test of significance does not

1

provide the information concerning psychological phenomena characteristically attributed to it; and that, furthermore, a great deal of mischief has been associated with its use. If the test of significance does not yield the expected information concerning the psychological phenomena under investigation, we may well speak of a crisis; for then a good deal of the research of the last several decades must be questioned. What will be said in this paper is hardly original. It is, in a certain sense, what "everybody knows." To say it "out loud" is, as it were, to assume the role of the child who pointed out that the emperor really had no clothes on. Little of what is contained in this paper is not already available in the literature, and the literature will be cited.

Lest what is being said here be misunderstood, some clarification needs to be made at the outset. It is not a blanket criticism of statistics, of mathematics, or, for that matter, even of the test of significance when it can be appropriately used, as in certain decision situations. The argument is rather that the test of significance has been carrying too much of the burden of scientific inference. It may well be the case that wise and ingenious investigators can find their way to reasonable conclusions from data because and in spite of their procedures. Too often, however, even wise and ingenious investigators, for varieties of reasons not the least of which are the editorial policies of our major psychological journals, which we will discuss below, tend to credit the test of significance with properties it does not have.

The test of significance has as its aim obtaining information concerning a characteristic of a *population* which is itself not directly observable, whether for practical or more intrinsic reasons. What is observable is the *sample*. The work assigned to the test of significance is that of aiding in making inferences from the observed sample to the unobserved population.

The critical assumption involved in testing significance is that, if the experiment is conducted properly, the characteristics of the population have a designably determinative influence on samples drawn from it; that, for example, the mean of a population

2

has a determinative influence on the mean of a sample drawn from it. Thus if P, the population characteristic, has a determinative influence on S, the sample characteristic, then there is some license for making inferences from S to P.

If the determinative influence of P on S could be put in the form of simple logical implication, that P implies S, the problem would be quite simple. For, then we would have the simple situation: if P implies S, and if S is false, P is false. There are some limited instances in which this logic applies directly in sampling. For example, if the range of values in the population is between 3 and 9 (P), then the range of values in any sample must be between 3 and 9 (S). Should we find a value in a sample of, say, 10, it would mean that S is false; and we could assert that P is false.

It is clear from this, however, that, strictly speaking, one can only go from the denial of S to the denial of P; and not from the assertion of S to the assertion of P. It is within this context of simple logical implication that the Fisher school of statisticians have made important contributions—and it is extremely important to recognize this as the context.

In contrast, approaches based on the theorem of Bayes (Edwards, Lindman, & Savage, 1963; Keynes, 1948; Savage, 1954; Schlaifer, 1959) would allow inferences to P from S even when S is not denied, as S adding something to the credibility of P when S is found to be the case. One of the most viable alternatives to the use of the test of significance involves the theorem of Bayes; and the paper by Edwards et al. (1963) is particularly directed to the attention of psychologists for use in psychological research.

The notion of the null hypothesis[1] promoted by Fisher

---

[1] There is some confusion in the literature concerning the meaning of the term "null hypothesis." Fisher used the term to designate any exact hypothesis that we might be interested in disproving, and "null" was used in the sense of that which is to be nullified (see, for example, Berkson, 1942). It has, however, also been used to indicate a parameter of zero (see, for example, Lindquist, 1940): the difference between the population

3

(1947) constituted an advance within this context of simple logical implication. It allowed experimenters to set up a null hypothesis complementary to the hypothesis that the investigator was interested in, and provided him with a way of positively confirming his hypothesis. Thus, for example, the investigator might have the hypothesis that, say, normals differ from schizophrenics. He would then set up the null hypothesis that the means in the population of all normals and all schizophrenics were equal. Thus, the rejection of the null hypothesis constituted a way of asserting that the means of the populations of normals and schizophrenics were different, a seemingly reasonable device whereby to affirm a logical antecedent.

The model of simple logical implication for making inferences from S to P has another difficulty which the Fisher approach sought to overcome. This is that it is rarely meaningful to set up any simple "P implies S" model for parameters that we are interested in. In the case of the mean, for example, it is rather that P has a determinative influence on the frequency of any specific S. But one experiment does not provide many values of S to allow the study of their frequencies. It gives us only one value of S. The sampling distribution is conceived which specifies the relative frequencies of all possible values of S. Then, with the help of an adopted level of significance, we could, in effect, say that S was false; that is, any S which fell in a region whose relative theoretical frequency under the null hypothesis was, say, 5 per cent would be considered false. If such an S actually occurred, we would be in a position to declare P to be false, still within the model of simple logical implication.

It is important to recognize that one of the essential features of the Fisher approach is what may be called the "once-ness" of the experiment; the inference model takes as critical that the experiment has been conducted once. If an S which has a low probability

---

means is zero, or the correlation coefficient in the population is zero, the difference in proportions in the population is zero, etc. Since both meanings are usually intended in psychological research, it causes little difficulty.

under the null hypothesis actually occurs, it is taken that the null hypothesis is false. As Fisher (1947) put it, why should the theoretically rare event under the null hypothesis actually occur to "us"? If it does occur, we take it that the null hypothesis is false. Basic is the idea that "the theoretically unusual does not happen to me."[2] It should be noted that the referent for all probability considerations is neither in the population itself nor the subjective confidence of the investigator. It is rather in a hypothetical population of experiments all conducted in the same manner, but only one of which is actually conducted. Thus, of course, the probability of falsely rejecting the null hypothesis if it were true is exactly that value which has been taken as the level of significance. Replication of the experiment vitiates the validity of the inference model, unless the replication itself is taken into account in the model and the probabilities of the model modified accordingly (as is done in various designs which entail replication, where, however, the total experiment, including the replications, is again considered as *one* experiment). According to Fisher (1947), "it is an essential characteristic of experimentation that it is carried out with limited resources." In the Fisher approach, the "limited resources" is not only a making of the best out of a limited situation, but is rather an integral feature of the inference model itself. Lest he be done a complete injustice, it should be pointed out that he did say, "In relation to the test of significance, we may say that a phenomenon is experimentally demonstrable when we know how to conduct an experiment which will rarely fail to give us statistically significant

[2] I playfully once conducted the following "experiment": Suppose, I said, that every coin has associated with it a "spirit"; and suppose, furthermore, that if the spirit is implored properly, the coin will veer head or tail as one requests of the spirit. I thus invoked the spirit to make the coin fall head. I threw it once; it came up head. I did it again; it came up head again. I did this six times, and got six heads. Under the null hypothesis the probability of occurrence of six heads is $(\frac{1}{2})^6 = .016$, significant at the 2 per cent level of significance. I have never repeated the experiment. But, then, the logic of the inference model does not really demand that I do! It may be objected that the coin, or my tossing, or even my observation was biased. But I submit that such things were in all likelihood not as involved in the result as corresponding things in most psychological research.

results." However, although Fisher "himself" believes this, it is not built into the inference model.[3]

As already indicated, research workers in the field of psychology place a heavy burden on the test of significance. Let us consider some of the difficulties associated with the null hypothesis.

1. *The a priori reasons for believing that the null hypothesis is generally false anyway.* One of the common experiences of research workers is the very high frequency with which significant results are obtained with large samples. Some years ago, the author had occasion to run a number of tests of significance on a battery of tests collected on about 60,000 subjects from all over the United States. Every test came out significant. Dividing the cards by such arbitrary criteria as east versus west of the Mississippi River, Maine versus the rest of the country, North versus South, etc., all produced significant differences in means. In some instances, the differences in the sample means were quite small, but nonetheless, the p values were all very low. Nunnally (1960) has reported a similar experience involving correlation coefficients on 700 subjects. Joseph Berkson (1938) made the observation almost 30 years ago in connection with chi-square:

> I believe that an observant statistician who has had any considerable experience with applying the chi-square test repeatedly will agree with my statement that, as a matter of observation, when the numbers in the data are quite large, the P's tend to come out small. Having observed this, and on reflection, I make the following dogmatic statement, referring for illustration to the normal curve: "If the normal curve is fitted to a body of data representing any real observations whatever of quantities in the physical world, then if the number of observations is extremely

[3] Possibly not even this criterion is sound. It may be that a number of statistically significant results which are borderline "speak for the null hypothesis rather than against it" (Edwards et al., 1963). If the null hypothesis were really false, then with an increase in the number of instances in which it can be rejected, there should be some substantial proportion of more dramatic rejections rather than borderline rejections.

6

large—for instance, on an order of 200,000—the chi-square *P* will be small beyond any usual limit of significance."

This dogmatic statement is made on the basis of an extrapolation of the observation referred to and can also be defended as a prediction from *a priori* considerations. For we may assume that it is practically certain that any series of real observations does not actually follow a normal curve *with absolute exactitude* in all respects, and no matter how small the discrepancy between the normal curve and the true curve of observations, the chi-square *P* will be small if the sample has a sufficiently large number of observations in it.

If this be so, then we have something here that is apt to trouble the conscience of a reflective statistician using the chi-square test. For I suppose it would be agreed by statisticians that a large sample is always better than a small sample. If, then, we know in advance the *P* that will result from an application of a chi-square test to a large sample, there would seem to be no use in doing it on a smaller one. But since the result of the former test is known, it is no test at all [pp. 526–527].

As one group of authors has put it, "in typical applications . . . the null hypothesis . . . is known by all concerned to be false from the outset" (Edwards, Lindman, and Savage, 1963). The fact of the matter is that there is really no good reason to expect the null hypothesis to be true in any population. Why should the mean, say, of all scores east of the Mississippi be identical to all scores west of the Mississippi? Why should any correlation coefficient be exactly .00 in the population? Why should we expect the ratio of males to females to be exactly 50:50 in any population? Or why should different drugs have exactly the same effect on any population parameter (Smith, 1960)? A glance at any set of statistics on total populations will quickly confirm the rarity of the null hypothesis in nature.

The reason the null hypothesis is characteristically rejected with large samples was made patent by the theoretical work of Neyman and Pearson (1933). The probability of rejecting the

7

null hypothesis is a function of five factors: whether the test is one- or two-tailed, the level of significance, the standard deviation, the amount of deviation from the null hypothesis, and the number of observations. The choice of a one- or two-tailed test is the investigator's; the level of significance is also based on the choice of the investigator; the standard deviation is a given of the situation and is characteristically reasonably well estimated; the deviation from the null hypothesis is what is unknown; and the choice of the number of cases in psychological work is characteristically arbitrary or expediential. Should there be any deviation from the null hypothesis in the population, no matter how small—and we have little doubt but that such a deviation usually exists—a sufficiently large number of observations will lead to the rejection of the null hypothesis. As Nunnally (1960) put it,

> if the null hypothesis is not rejected, it is usually because the N is too small. If enough data are gathered, the hypothesis will generally be rejected. If rejection of the null hypothesis were the real intention in psychological experiments, there usually would be no need to gather data [p. 643].

2. *Type I error and publication practices.* The Type I error is the error of rejecting the null hypothesis when it is indeed true, and its probability is the level of significance. Later in this paper we will discuss the distinction between sharp and loose null hypotheses. The sharp null hypothesis, which we have been discussing, is an exact value for the null hypothesis as, for example, the difference between population means being precisely zero. A loose null hypothesis is one in which it is conceived of as being "around" null. Sharp null hypotheses, as we have indicated, rarely exist in nature. Assuming that loose null hypotheses are not rare, and that their testing may make sense under some circumstances, let us consider the role of the publication practices of our journals in their connection.

It is the practice of editors of our psychological journals, receiving many more papers than they can possibly publish, to use

8

the magnitude of the p values reported as one criterion for acceptance or rejection of a study. For example, consider the following statement made by Arthur W. Melton (1962) on completing twelve years as editor of the *Journal of Experimental Psychology,* certainly one of the most prestigious and scientifically meticulous psychological journals. In listing the criteria by which articles were evaluated, he said:

> The next step in the assessment of an article involved a judgment with respect to the confidence to be placed in the findings —confidence that the results of the experiment would be repeatable under the conditions described. In editing the *Journal* there has been a strong reluctance to accept and publish results related to the principal concern of the research when those results were significant at the .05 level, whether by one- or two-tailed test. This has not implied a slavish worship of the .01 level, as some critics may have implied. Rather, it reflects a belief that it is the responsibility of the investigator in a science to reveal his effect in such a way that no reasonable man would be in a position to discredit the results by saying that they were the product of the way the ball bounces [pp. 553–554].

His clearly expressed opinion that nonsignificant results should not take up the space of the journals is shared by most editors of psychological journals. It is important to point out that I am not advocating a change in policy in this connection. In the total research enterprise where so much of the load for making inferences concerning the nature of phenomena is carried by the test of significance, the editors can do little else. The point is rather that the situation in regard to publication makes manifest the difficulties in connection with the overemphasis on the test of significance as a principal basis for making inferences.

McNemar (1960) has rightly pointed out that not only do journal editors reject papers in which the results are not significant, but that papers in which significance has not been obtained are not submitted, that investigators select out their significant findings for inclusion in their reports, and that theory-oriented research workers tend to discard data which do not work to confirm their theories. The result of all of this is that "published results are more likely to involve false rejection of null hypotheses than indicated by the stated levels of significance," that is, published results which are significant may well have Type I errors in them far in excess of, say, the 5 per cent which we may allow ourselves.

The suspicion that the Type I error may well be plaguing our literature is given confirmation in an analysis of articles published in the *Journal of Abnormal and Social Psychology* for one complete year (Cohen, 1962). Analyzing seventy studies in which significant results were obtained with respect to the power of the statistical tests used, Cohen found that power, the probability of rejecting the null hypothesis when the null hypothesis was false, was characteristically meager. Theoretically, with such tests, one should not often expect significant results even when the null hypothesis was false. Yet, there they were! Even if deviations from null existed in the relevant populations, the investigations were characteristically not powerful enough to have detected them. This strongly suggests that there is something additional associated with these rejections of the null hypotheses in question. It strongly points to the possibility that the manner in which studies get published is associated with the findings; that the very publication practices themselves are part and parcel of the probabilistic processes on which we base our conclusions concerning the nature of psychological phenomena. Our total research enterprise is, at least in part, a kind of scientific roulette, in which the "lucky," or constant player, "wins," that is, gets his paper or papers published. And certainly, going from 5 per cent to 1 per cent does not eliminate the possibility that it is "the way the ball bounces," to use Melton's phrase. It changes the odds in this roulette, but it does not make it less a game of roulette.

The damage to the scientific enterprise is compounded by the fact that the publication of "significant" results tends to stop further investigation. If the publication of papers containing Type I errors tended to foster further investigation so that the psychological phenomena with which we are concerned would be further probed

10

by others, it would not be too bad. But it does not. Quite the contrary. As Lindquist (1940) has correctly pointed out, the danger to science of the Type I error is much more serious than the Type II error—for when a Type I error is committed, it has the effect of stopping investigation. A highly significant result appears definitive, as Melton's comments indicate. In the twelve years that he edited the *Journal of Experimental Psychology,* he sought to select papers which were worthy of being placed in the "archives," as he put it. Even the strict repetition of an experiment and not getting significance in the same way does not speak against the result already reported in the literature. For failing to get significance, speaking strictly within the inference model, only means that that experiment is inconclusive; whereas the study already reported in the literature, with a low p value, is regarded as conclusive. Thus we tend to place in the archives studies with a relatively high number of Type I errors, or, at any rate, studies which reflect small deviations from null in the respective populations; and we act in such a fashion as to reduce the likelihood of their correction. From time to time the suggestion has arisen that journals should open their pages for "negative results," so called. What is characteristically meant is that the null hypothesis has not been rejected at a conventional level of significance. This is hardly a solution to the problem simply because a failure to reject the null hypothesis is not a "negative result." It is only an instance in which the experiment is inconclusive.

To make this point clearer let us consider the odd case in which the null hypothesis may actually be true; say, the difference between means of a given measure of two identifiable groups in the population is precisely zero. Let us imagine that over the world there are one hundred experimenters who have independently embarked on testing this particular null hypothesis. By the theory under which the whole test of significance is conceived, approximately ninety-five of these experimenters would wind up by not being able to reject the null hypothesis, that is, their results would not be significant. It is not likely that they would write up their experiments and submit them to any journals. However, approxi-

11

mately five of these experimenters would find that their observed difference in means is significant at the 5 per cent level of significance. It is likely that they would write up their experiments and submit them for publication. Indeed, one might imagine interesting quarrels arising among them concerning priority of discovery, if the differences came out in the same direction, and controversy, if the differences came out in different directions. In the former instance, the psychological community might even take it as evidence of "replicability" of the phenomenon, in the latter instance as evidence that the scientific method is "self-corrective." The other ninety-five experimenters would wonder what they did wrong. And this is in the odd instance in which the true difference between means in the population is precisely zero!

The psychological literature is filled with misinterpretations of the nature of the test of significance. One may be tempted to attribute this to such things as lack of proper education, the simple fact that humans may err, and the prevailing tendency to take a cookbook approach in which the mathematical and philosophical framework out of which the tests of significance emerge are ignored; that, in other words, these misinterpretations are somehow the result of simple intellectual inadequacy on the part of psychologists. However, such an explanation is hardly tenable. Graduate schools are adamant with respect to statistical education. Any number of psychologists have taken out substantial amounts of time to equip themselves mathematically and philosophically. Psychologists as a group do a great deal of mutual criticism. Editorial reviews prior to publication are carried out with eminent conscientiousness. There is even a substantial literature devoted to various kinds of "misuse" of statistical procedures, to which not a little attention has been paid.

It is rather that the test of significance is profoundly interwoven with other strands of the psychological research enterprise in such a way that it constitutes a critical part of the total cultural-scientific tapestry. To pull out the strand of the test of significance would seem to make the whole tapestry fall apart. In the face of the intrinsic difficulties that the test of significance provides, we

12

rather attempt to make an "adjustment" by attributing to the test of significance characteristics which it does not have, and overlook characteristics that it does have. The difficulty is that the test of significance can, especially when not considered too carefully, do *some* work; for, after all, the results of the test of significance *are* related to the phenomena in which we are interested. One may well ask whether we do not have here, perhaps, an instance of the phenomenon that learning under partial reinforcement is very highly resistant to extinction. Some of these misinterpretations are as follows:

1. *Taking the p value as a "measure" of significance.* A common misinterpretation of the test of significance is to regard it as a "measure" of significance. It is interpreted as the answer to the question "How significant is it?" A p value of .05 is thought of as less significant than a p value of .01, and so on. The characteristic practice on the part of psychologists is to compute, say, a t, and then "look up" the significance in the table, taking the p value as a function of t, and thereby a "measure" of significance. Indeed, since the p value is inversely related to the magnitude of, say, the difference between means in the sample, it can function as a kind of "standard score" measure for a variety of different experiments. Mathematically, the t is actually very similar to a "standard score," entailing a deviation in the numerator, and a function of the variation in the denominator; and the p value is a "function" of t. If this use were explicit, it, would perhaps not be too bad. But it must be remembered that this is using the p value as a statistic descriptive of the sample alone, and does not automatically give an inference to the population. There is even the practice of using tests of significance in studies of total populations, in which the observations cannot by any stretch of the imagination be thought of as having been randomly selected from any designable population.[4] Using the p value in this way, in which the statistical inference

[4] It was decided not to cite any specific studies to exemplify points such as this one. The reader will undoubtedly be able to supply them for himself.

model is even hinted at, is completely indefensible; for the single function of the statistical inference model is making inferences to populations from samples.

The practice of "looking up" the p value for the t, which has even been advocated in some of our statistical handbooks (e.g., Lacey, 1953; Underwood et al., 1954), rather than looking up the t for a given p value, violates the inference model. The inference model is based on the presumption that one initially adopts a level of significance as the specification of that probability which is too low to occur to "us," as Fisher has put it, in this one instance, and under the null hypothesis. A purist might speak of the "delicate problem . . . of fudging with a posteriori alpha values [levels of significance]" (Kaiser, 1960), as though the levels of significance were initially decided upon, but rarely do psychological research workers or editors take the level of significance as other than a "measure."

But taken as a "measure," it is only a measure of the sample. Psychologists often erroneously believe that the p value is "the probability that the results are due to chance," as Wilson (1961) has pointed out; that a p value of .05 means that the chances are .95 that the scientific hypothesis is correct, as Bolles (1962) has pointed out; that it is a measure of the power to "predict" the behavior of a population (Underwood et al., 1954); and that it is a measure of the "confidence that the results of the experiment would be repeatable under the conditions described," as Melton (1962) put it. Unfortunately, none of these interpretations are within the inference model of the test of significance. Some of our statistical handbooks have "allowed" misinterpretation. For example, in discussing the erroneous rhetoric associated with talking of the "probability" of a population parameter (in the inference model there is no probability associated with something which is either true or false), Lindquist (1940) said, "For most practical purposes, the end result is the same as if the 'level of confidence' type of interpretation is employed." Ferguson (1959) wrote, "The .05 and .01 probability levels are descriptive of our degree of confidence." There is little question but that sizable differences, corre-

14

lations, etc., in samples, especially samples of reasonable size, speak more strongly of sizable differences, correlations, etc., in the population; and there is little question but that if there is real and strong effect in the population, it will continue to manifest itself in further sampling. However, these are inferences which *we* may make. They are outside the inference model associated with the test of significance. The p value within the inference model is only the value which we take to be as how improbable an event could be under the null hypothesis, which we judge will not take place to "us," in this one experiment. It is not a "measure" of the goodness of the other inferences which we might make. It is an a priori condition that we set up whereby we decide whether or not we will reject the null hypothesis, not a measure of significance.

There is a study in the literature (Rosenthal and Gaito, 1963) which points up sharply the lack of understanding on the part of psychologists of the meaning of the test of significance. The subjects were nine members of the psychology department faculty, all holding doctoral degrees, and ten graduate students, at the University of North Dakota; and there is little reason to believe that this group of psychologists was more or less sophisticated than any other. They were asked to rate their degree of belief or confidence in results of hypothetical studies for a variety of p values, and for N's of 10 and 100. That there should be a relationship between the average rated confidence or belief and p value, as they found, is to be expected. What is shocking is that these psychologists indicated substantially greater confidence or belief in results associated with the larger sample size for the same p values. According to the theory, especially as this has been amplified by Neyman and Pearson (1933), the probability of rejecting the null hypothesis for any given deviation from null and p value increases as a function of the number of observations. The rejection of the null hypothesis when the number of cases is small speaks for a more dramatic effect in the population; and if the p value is the same, the probability of committing a Type I error remains the same. Thus one can be more confident with a small N than a large N. The question is, how could a group of psychologists be so wrong? I believe that this wrongness is based on the commonly held belief that the p value is a "measure" of degree of confidence. Thus, the reasoning behind such a wrong set of answers by these psychologists may well have been something like this: the p value is a measure of confidence; but a larger number of cases also increases confidence; therefore, for any given p value, the degree of confidence should be higher for the larger N. The wrong conclusion arises from the erroneous character of the first premise, and from the failure to recognize that the p value is a function of sample size for any given deviation from null in the population. The author knows of instances in which editors of very reputable psychological journals have rejected papers in which the p values and N's were small on the grounds that there were not enough observations, clearly demonstrating that the same mode of thought is operating in them. Indeed, rejecting the null hypothesis with a small N is indicative of a strong deviation from null in the population, the mathematics of the test of significance having already taken into account the smallness of the sample. Increasing the N increases the probability of rejecting the null hypothesis; and in these studies rejected for small sample size, that task has already been accomplished. These editors are, of course, in some sense the ultimate "teachers" of the profession; and they have been teaching something which is patently wrong.

2. *Automaticity of inference.* What may be considered to be a dream, fantasy, or ideal in the culture of psychology is that of achieving complete automaticity of inference. The making of inductive generalizations is always somewhat risky. In Fisher's *The Design of Experiments* (1947), he made the claim that the methods of induction could be made rigorous, exemplified by the procedures which he was setting forth. This is indeed quite correct in the sense indicated earlier. In a later paper (Fisher, 1955), he made explicit what was strongly hinted at in his earlier writing, that the methods which he proposed constituted a relatively complete specification of the process of induction:

That such a process induction existed and was possible to normal minds, has been understood for centuries; it is only with the recent development of statistical science that an analytic account can now be given, about as satisfying and complete, at least, as that given traditionally of the deductive processes [p. 74].

Psychologists certainly took the procedures associated with the *t* test, *F* test, and so on, in this manner. Instead of having to engage in inference themselves, they had but to "run the tests" for the purpose of making inferences, since, as it appeared, the statistical tests were analytic analogues of inductive inference. The "operationist" orientation among psychologists, which recognized the contingency of knowledge on the knowledge-getting operations and advocated their specification, could, it would seem, "operationalize" the inferential processes simply by reporting the details of the statistical analysis. It thus removed the burden of responsibility, the chance of being wrong, the necessity for making inductive inferences, from the shoulders of the investigator and placed them on the tests of significance. The contingency of the conclusion upon the experimenter's decision of the level of significance was managed in two ways. The first, by resting on a kind of social agreement that 5 per cent was good, and 1 per cent better. The second in the manner which has already been discussed, by not making a decision of the level of significance, but only reporting the *p* value as a "result" and a presumably objective "measure" of degree of confidence. But that the probability of getting significance is also contingent upon the number of observations has been handled largely by ignoring it.

A crisis was experienced among psychologists when the matter of the one- versus the two-tailed test came into prominence; for here the contingency of the result of a test of significance on a decision of the investigator was simply too conspicuous to be ignored. An investigator, say, was interested in the difference between two groups on some measure. He collected his data, found that Mean A was greater than Mean B in the sample, and ran the ordinary two-tailed *t* test; and, let us say, it was not significant. Then he bethought himself. The two-tailed test tested against *two*

17

alternatives, that the population Mean A was greater than population Mean B and vice versa. But then, he really wanted to know whether Mean A was greater than Mean B. Thus, he could run a one-tailed test. He did this and found, since the one-tailed test is more powerful, that his difference was now significant.

Now here there was a difficulty. The test of significance is not nearly so automatic an inference process as had been thought. It is manifestly contingent on the decision of the investigator as to whether to run a one- or a two-tailed test. And, somehow, making the decision *after* the data were collected and the means computed seemed like "cheating." How should this be handled? Should there be some central registry in which one registers one's decision to run a one- or two-tailed test before collecting the data? Should one, as one eminent psychologist once suggested to me, send oneself a letter so that the postmark would prove that one had predecided to run a one-tailed test? The literature on ways of handling this difficulty has grown quite a bit in the strain to overcome somehow this particular clear contingency of the results of a test of significance on the decision of the investigator. The author will not attempt here to review this literature, except to cite one very competent paper which points up the intrinsic difficulty associated with this problem, the *reductio ad absurdum* to which one comes. Kaiser (1960), early in his paper, distinguished between the logic associated with the test of significance and other forms of inference, a distinction which, incidentally, Fisher would hardly have allowed: "The arguments developed in this paper are based on logical considerations in statistical inference. (We do not, of course, suggest that statistical inference is the only basis for scientific inference.)" But then, having taken the position that he is going to follow the logic of statistical inference relentlessly, he said (Kaiser's italics): *"we cannot logically make a directional statistical decision or statement when the null hypothesis is rejected on the basis of the direction of the difference in the observed sample means."* One really needs to strike oneself in the head! If Sample Mean A is greater than Sample Mean B, and there is reason to reject the null hypothesis, in what other direction can it reasonably be? What kind of logic

18

is it that leads one to believe that it could be otherwise than that Population Mean A is greater than Population Mean B? We do not know whether Kaiser intended his paper as a *reductio ad absurdum*, but it certainly turned out that way.

The issue of the one- versus the two-tailed test genuinely challenges the presumptive "objectivity" characteristically attributed to the test of significance. On the one hand, it makes patent what was the case under any circumstances (at the least in the choice of level of significance, and the choice of the number of cases in the sample), that the conclusion is contingent upon the decision of the investigator. An astute investigator, who foresaw the results, and who therefore predecided to use a one-tailed test, will get one p value. The less astute but honorable investigator, who did not foresee the results, would feel obliged to use a two-tailed test, and would get another p value. On the other hand, if one decides to be relentlessly logical within the logic of statistical inference, one winds up with the kind of absurdity which we have cited above.

3. *The confusion of induction to the aggregate with induction to the general* (see pages 30–36 below). Consider a not atypical investigation of the following sort: A group of, say, twenty normals and a group of, say, twenty schizophrenics are given a test. The tests are scored, and a t test is run, and it is found that the means differ significantly at some level of significance, say 1 per cent. What inference can be drawn? As we have already indicated, the investigator could have insured this result by choosing a sufficiently large number of cases. Suppose we overlook this objection, which we can to some extent, by saying that the difference between the means in the population must have been large enough to have manifested itself with only forty cases. But still, what do we know from this? The only inference which this allows is that the mean of all normals is different from the mean of all schizophrenics in the populations from which the samples have presumably been drawn at random. (Rarely is the criterion of randomness satisfied. But let us overlook this objection too.)

The common rhetoric in which such results are discussed is

in the form "Schizophrenics differ from normals in such and such ways." The sense that both the reader and the writer have of this rhetoric is that it has been justified by the finding of significance. Yet clearly it does not mean *all* schizophrenics and *all* normals. All that the test of significance justifies is that measures of central tendency of the aggregates differ in the populations. The test of significance has *not* addressed itself to anything about the schizophrenia or normality which characterizes *each* member of the respective populations. Now it is certainly possible for an investigator to develop a hypothesis about the nature of schizophrenia from which he may infer that there should be differences between the means in the populations; and his finding of a significant difference in the means of his sample would add to the credibility of the former. However, that 1 per cent which he obtained in his study bears only on the means of the populations and is not a "measure" of the confidence that he may have in his hypothesis concerning the nature of schizophrenia. There are two inferences that he must make. One is that of the sample to the population, for which the test of significance is of some use. The other is from his inference concerning the population to his hypothesis concerning the nature of schizophrenia. The p value does not bear on this second inference. The psychological literature is filled with assertions which confound these two inferential processes.

Or consider another hardly atypical style of research. Say an experimenter divides forty subjects at random into two groups of twenty subjects each. One group is assigned to one condition and the other to another condition, perhaps, say, massing and distribution of trials. The subjects are given a learning task, one group under massed conditions, the other under distributed conditions. The experimenter runs a t test on the learning measure and again, say, finds that the difference is significant at the 1 per cent level of significance. He may then say in his report, being more careful than the psychologist who was studying the difference between normals and schizophrenics (being more "scientific" than his clinically interested colleague), that "the mean in the population of learning under massed conditions is lower than the mean in the population of learning under distributed conditions," feeling that he can say this with a good deal of certainty because of his test of significance. But here too (like his clinical colleague) he has made two inferences, and not one, and the 1 per cent bears on the one but not the other. The statistical inference model certainly allows him to make his statement for the population, but only for *that* learning task, and the *p* value is appropriate only to that. But the generalization to "massed conditions" and "distributed conditions" beyond that particular learning task is a second inference with respect to which the *p* value is not relevant. The psychological literature is plagued with any number of instances in which the rhetoric indicates that the p value does bear on this second inference.

Part of the blame for this confusion can be ascribed to Fisher who, in *The Design of Experiments* (1947), suggested that the mathematical methods which he proposed were exhaustive of scientific induction, and that the principles he was advancing were "common to all experimentation." What he failed to see and to say was that after an inference was made concerning a population parameter, one still needed to engage in induction to obtain meaningful scientific propositions.

To regard the methods of statistical inference as exhaustive of the inductive inferences called for in experimentation is completely confounding. When the test of significance has been run, the necessity for induction has hardly been completely satisfied. However, the research worker knows this, in some sense, and proceeds, as he should, to make further inductive inferences. He is, however, still ensnarled in his test of significance and the presumption that it is the whole of his inductive activity, and thus mistakenly takes a low *p* value for the measure of the validity of his other inductions.

The seriousness of this confusion may be seen by again referring back to the Rosenthal and Gaito study and the remark by Berkson which indicate that research workers believe that a large sample is better than a small sample. We need to refine the rhetoric somewhat. Induction consists in making inferences from the particular to the general. It is certainly the case that, as confirming particulars are added, the credibility of the general is increased. However, the addition of observations to a sample is, in the context of statistical inference, not the addition of particulars but the modification of what is one particular in the inference model, the sample aggregate. In the context of statistical inference, it is not necessarily true that "a large sample is better than a small sample." For, as has been already indicated, obtaining a significant result with a small sample suggests a larger deviation from null in the population, and may be considerably more meaningful. Thus more particulars are better than fewer particulars in the making of an inductive inference; but not necessarily a larger sample.

In the marriage of psychological research and statistical inference, psychology brought its own reasons for accepting this confusion, reasons which inhere in the history of psychology. Measurement psychology arises out of two radically different traditions, as has been pointed out by Guilford (1936) and Cronbach (1957), and the matter of putting them together raised certain difficulties. The one tradition seeks to find propositions concerning the nature of man in general—propositions of a general nature, with each individual a particular in which the general is manifest. This is the kind of psychology associated with the traditional experimental psychology of Fechner, Ebbinghaus, Wundt, and Titchener. It seeks to find the laws which characterize the "generalized, normal, human, adult mind" (Boring, 1950). The research strategy associated with this kind of psychology is straightforwardly inductive. It seeks inductive generalizations which will apply to every member of a designated class. A single particular in which a generalization fails forces a rejection of the generalization, calling for either a redefinition of the class to which it applies or a modification of the generalization. The other tradition is the psychology of individual differences, which has its roots more in England and the United States than on the Continent. We may recall that when the young American, James McKeen Cattell, who invented the term "mental test," came to Wundt with his own problem of individual differences, it was regarded by Wundt as *ganz Amerkanisch* (Boring, 1950).

22

The basic datum for an individual-differences approach is not anything that characterizes each of two subjects, but the difference between them. For this latter tradition, it is the aggregate which is of interest, and not the general. One of the most unfortunate characteristics of many studies in psychology, especially in experimental psychology, is that the data are treated as aggregates while the experimenter is trying to infer general propositions. There is hardly an issue of most of the major psychological journals reporting experimentation in which this confusion does not appear several times, and in which the test of significance, which has some value in connection with the study of aggregates, is not interpreted as a measure of the credibility of the general proposition in which the investigator is interested. Roberts and Wist examined sixty articles from psychological literature from the point of view of the aggregate-general distinction. In twenty-five of the articles it was unambiguous that the authors had drawn general-type conclusions from aggregate-type data.

Thus, what took place historically in psychology is that instead of attempting to synthesize the two traditional approaches to psychological phenomena, which is both possible and desirable, a syncretic combination took place of the methods appropriate to the study of aggregates with the aims of a psychology which sought for general propositions. One of the most overworked terms, which added not a little to the essential confusion, was "error," which was a kind of umbrella term for (at the least) variation among scores from different individuals, variation among measurements for the same individual, and variation among samples.

Let us add another historical note. In 1936, Guilford published his well-known *Psychometric Methods*. In this book, which became a kind of "bible" for many psychologists, he made a noble effort at a "Rapprochement of Psychophysical and Test Methods." He observed, quite properly, that mathematical developments in each of the two fields might be of value in the other, that "Both psychophysics and mental testing have rested upon the same fundamental statistical devices." There is no question of the truth of this. However, what he failed to emphasize sufficiently was that mathematics is so abstract that the same mathematics is applicable to rather different fields of investigation without there being any necessary further identity between them. (One would not, for example, argue that business and genetics are essentially the same because the same arithmetic is applicable to market research and in the investigation of the facts of heredity.) A critical point of contact between the two traditions was in connection with scaling, in which Cattell's principle that "equally often noticed differences are equal unless always or never noticed" (Guilford, 1936) was adopted as a fundamental assumption. The "equally often noticed differences" is, of course, based on aggregates. By means of this assumption, one could collapse the distinction between the two areas of investigation. Indeed, this is not really too bad if one is alert to the fact that it is an assumption, one which even has considerable pragmatic value. As a set of techniques whereby data could be analyzed, that is, as a set of techniques whereby one could describe one's findings, and then make inductions about the nature of the psychological phenomena, what Guilford put together in his book was eminently valuable. However, around this time the work of Fisher and his school was coming to the attention of psychologists. It was attractive for several reasons. It offered advice for handling "small samples." It offered a number of eminently ingenious new ways of organizing and extracting information from data. It offered ways by which several variables could be analyzed simultaneously, away from the old notion that one had to keep everything constant and vary only one variable at a time. It showed how the effect of the "interaction" of variables could be assessed. But it also claimed to have mathematized induction! The Fisher approach was thus "bought," and psychologists got a theory of induction in the bargain, a theory which seemed to exhaust the inductive processes. Whereas the question of the "reliability" of statistics had been a matter of concern for some time before (although frequently very garbled), it had not carried the burden of induction to the degree that it did with the Fisher approach. With the acceptance of the Fisher approach the psychological research worker also accepted, and then overused, the test of significance, employing it as the measure of the significance, in the largest sense of the word, of his research efforts.

Earlier, a distinction was made between sharp and loose null hypotheses. One of the major difficulties associated with the Fisher approach is the problem presented by sharp null hypotheses; for, as we have already seen, there is reason to believe that the existence of sharp null hypotheses is characteristically unlikely. There have been some efforts to correct for this difficulty by proposing the use of loose null hypotheses; in place of a single point, a region being considered null. Hodges and Lehmann (1954) have proposed a distinction between "statistical significance," which entails the sharp hypothesis, and "material significance," in which one tests the hypothesis of a deviation of a stated amount from the null point instead of the null point itself. Edwards (1950) has suggested the notion of "practical significance" in which one takes into account the meaning, in some practical sense, of the magnitude of the deviation from null together with the number of observations which have been involved in getting statistical significance. Binder (1963) has equally argued that a subset of parameters be equated with the null hypothesis. Essentially what has been suggested is that the investigator make some kind of a decision concerning "How much, say, of a difference makes a difference?" The difficulty with this solution, which is certainly a sound one technically, is that in psychological research we do not often have very good grounds for answering this question. This is partly due to the inadequacies of psychological measurement, but mostly due to the fact that the answer to the question of "How much of a difference makes a difference?" is not forthcoming outside of some particular practical context. The question calls forth another question, "How much of a difference makes a difference *for what?*"

This brings us to one of the major issues within the field of statistics itself. The problems of the research psychologist do not generally lie within practical contexts. He is rather interested in making assertions concerning psychological functions which have a

25

reasonable amount of credibility associated with them. He is more concerned with "What is the case?" than with "What is wise to do?" (see Rozeboom, 1960).

It is here that the decision-theory approach of Neyman, Pearson, and Wald (Neyman, 1937, 1957; Neyman & Pearson, 1933; Wald, 1939, 1950, 1955) becomes relevant. The decision-theory school, still basing itself on some basic notions of the Fisher approach, deviated from it in several respects:

1. In Fisher's inference model, the two alternatives between which one chose on the basis of an experiment were "reject" and "inconclusive." As he said in *The Design of Experiments* (1947), "the null hypothesis is never proved or established, but is possibly disproved, in the course of experimentation." In the decision-theory approach, the two alternatives are rather "reject" and "accept."

2. Whereas in the Fisher approach the interpretation of the test of significance critically depends on having one sample from a hypothetical population of experiments, the decision-theory approach conceives of, is applicable to, and is sensible with respect to numerous repetitions of the experiment.

3. The decision-theory approach added the notions of the Type II error (which can be made only if the null hypothesis is accepted) and power as significant features of their model.

4. The decision-theory model gave a significant place to the matter of what is concretely lost if an error is made in the practical context, on the presumption that "accept" entailed one concrete action, and "reject" another. It is in these actions and their consequences that there is a basis for deciding on a level of confidence. The Fisher approach has little to say about the consequences.

As it has turned out, the field of application par excellence for the decision-theory approach has been the sampling inspection of mass-produced items. In sampling inspection, the acceptable deviation from null can be specified; both "accept" and "reject" are appropriate categories; the alternative courses of action can be clearly specified; there is a definite measure of loss for each possible action; and the choice can be regarded as one of a series of such choices, so that one can minimize the over-all loss (see Barnard,

26

1954). Where the aim is only the acquisition of knowledge without regard to a specific practical context, these conditions do not often prevail. Many psychologists who learned about analysis of variance from books such as those by Snedecor (1946) found the examples involving hog weights, etc., somewhat annoying. The decision-theory school makes it clear that such practical contexts are not only "examples" given for pedagogical purposes, but actually are essential features of the methods themselves.

The contributions of the decision-theory school essentially revealed the intrinsic nature of the test of significance beyond that seen by Fisher and his colleagues. They demonstrated that the methods associated with the test of significance constitute not an assertion, or an induction, or a conclusion calculus, but a decision- or risk-evaluation calculus. Fisher (1955) has reacted to the decision-theory approach in polemic style, suggesting that its advocates were like "Russians [who] are made familiar with the ideal that research in pure science can and should be geared to technological performance, in the comprehensive organized effort of a five-year plan for the nation." He also suggested an American "ideological" orientation: "In the U. S. also the great importance of organized technology has I think made it easy to confuse the process appropriate for drawing correct conclusions, with those aimed rather at, let us say, speeding production, or saving money."[5] But perhaps a more reasonable way of looking at this is to regard the decision-theory school to have explicated what was already implicit in the work of the Fisher school.

What then is our alternative, if the test of significance is really of such limited appropriateness? At the very least it would appear that we would be much better off if we were to attempt to estimate the magnitude of the parameters in the populations; and recognize that we then need to make other inferences concerning the psychological phenomena which may be manifesting themselves in these magnitudes. In terms of a statistical approach which is an alternative, the various methods associated with the theorem of

[5] For a reply to Fisher, see Pearson (1955).

Bayes, referred to earlier, may be appropriate; and the paper by Edwards, Lindman, and Savage (1963) and the book by Schlaifer (1959) are good starting points. However, what is expressed in the theorem of Bayes alludes to the more general process of inducing propositions concerning the nonmanifest (which is what the population is a special instance of) and ascertaining the way in which what is manifest (of which the sample is a special instance) bears on it. This is what the scientific method has been about for centuries. However, if the reader who might be sympathetic to the considerations set forth in this paper quickly goes out and reads some of the material on the Bayesian approach with the hope that thereby he will find a new basis for automatic inference, this paper will have misfired, and he will be disappointed.

What we have indicated in this paper in connection with the test of significance in psychological research may be taken as an instance of a kind of essential mindlessness in the conduct of research which may be related to the presumption of the nonexistence of mind in the subjects of psychological research. Karl Pearson once indicated that higher statistics was only common sense reduced to numerical appreciation. However, that base in common sense must be maintained with vigilance. When we reach a point where our statistical procedures are substitutes instead of aids to thought, and we are led to absurdities, then we must return to common sense. Tukey (1962) has very properly pointed out that statistical procedures may take our attention away from the data, which constitute the ultimate base for any inferences which we might make. Schlaifer (1959) has dubbed the error of the misapplication of statistical procedures the "error of the third kind," the most serious error which can be made. Berkson has suggested the use of "the interocular traumatic test, you know what the data mean when the conclusion hits you between the eyes" (Edwards et al., 1963). We must overcome the myth that if our treatment of our subject matter is mathematical it is therefore precise and valid. We need to overcome the handicap associated with limited competence in mathematics, a competence that makes it possible for us to run tests of significance while it intimidates us with a vision of greater mathematical competence if only one could reach up to it. Mathematics can serve to obscure as well as reveal.

Most important, we need to get on with the business of generating psychological hypotheses and proceed to do investigations and make inferences which bear on them, instead of, as so much of our literature would attest, testing the statistical null hypothesis in any number of contexts in which we have every reason to suppose that it is false in the first place.

Group and
Individual Functions

A paper by Sidman (1952) has indicated a devastating criticism of a great deal of current and historical psychological research. He has demonstrated in the particular case of Hull's exponential growth function that if the functional relationship between two variables, x and y, for any particular individual is

$$y = f(x) \qquad [1]$$

then the average y-value, $\bar{y}$, is of the form

$$\bar{y} = g(x) \qquad [2]$$

where g (x) may be a fundamentally different equation from f (x). He shows that if the learning curve for an individual is

$$y = M - Me^{-kx} \tag{3}$$

then the form of the function based on the average y is not necessarily the same as [3].

Sidman indicates that the kind of analysis he has made can be applied to any function. In this paper we attempt to generalize Sidman's results for any functional relationship, and to provide a criterion for deciding on the legitimacy of the averaging operation as a device for making inferences concerning individual functional relationships.

The major tool that we avail ourselves of is the Maclaurin series:

$$f(x) = f(0) + xf'(0) + \frac{x^2}{2!}f''(0) + \frac{x^3}{3!}f'''(0) + \cdots \tag{4}$$

where $f(x)$ is our function, $f(0)$ is the value of the function when $x = 0$, $f'(0)$ is the value of the first derivative of the function when $x = 0$, etc.

Thus, if

$$y = f(a, b, c, \cdots, x) \tag{5}$$

for a particular individual, then

$$\bar{y} = \frac{\Sigma y}{n} = \frac{\Sigma f(a, b, c, \cdots, x)}{n}. \tag{6}$$

Applying the Maclaurin series, we get

$$y = y_0 + y_0'x + y_0''\frac{x^2}{2!} + y_0'''\frac{x^3}{3!} + \cdots \tag{7}$$

and

$$\bar{y} = \bar{y}_0 + \bar{y}_0'x + \bar{y}_0''\frac{x^2}{2!} + \bar{y}_0'''\frac{x^3}{3!} + \cdots \tag{8}$$

31

The criterion which we offer to determine the legitimacy of the averaging operation as a basis for making inferences concerning individual functional relationships is as follows: If the coefficients $\bar{y}_0$, $\bar{y}_0'$, $\bar{y}_0''$, etc., are simply functions of the average parameters, $\bar{a}$, $\bar{b}$, $\bar{c}$, etc., then the operation may be considered legitimate. When this criterion is satisfied, the form of the average curve will be identical with the form of each individual curve. It will differ from the individual curves only in the parameters of the function. When the criterion is satisfied the parameter of the group function will be related to the parameter of any individual function in the same way that any mean is related to any individual score. If we restrict ourselves to functions which satisfy the criterion, we may then make inferences concerning the nature of individual functions from the nature of group functions, since the functions will have the same form.

To demonstrate the application of the criterion we will examine two functions

$$y = ax^2 + bx + c \qquad [9]$$

and

$$y = M - Me^{-kx}. \qquad [10]$$

If $y = ax^2 + bx + c$, then

$$
\begin{aligned}
& & y_0 &= c \\
y' &= 2ax + b & y_0' &= b \\
y'' &= 2a & y_0'' &= 2a.
\end{aligned}
\qquad [11]
$$

Therefore, applying [7] and [8], we find

$$y = c + bx + ax^2 \qquad [12]$$

for the individual, and

$$\bar{y} = \bar{c} + \bar{b}x + \bar{a}x^2 \qquad [13]$$

for the group. Thus, the criterion is satisfied and we can consider the averaging a legitimate operation.

If, however, $y = M - Me^{-kx}$, then

$$y_0 = 0$$

$$y' = Mke^{-kx} \qquad y_0' = Mk$$

$$y'' = -Mk^2e^{-kx} \qquad y_0'' = -Mk^2 \qquad [14]$$

$$y''' = Mk^3e^{-kx} \qquad y_0''' = Mk^3$$

$$\vdots \qquad\qquad \vdots$$

Applying [7] and [8], we find

$$y = 0 + Mkx - Mk^2\frac{x^2}{2!} + Mk^3\frac{x^3}{3!} - \cdots \qquad [15]$$

and

$$\bar{y} = 0 + \overline{(Mk)}x - \overline{(Mk^2)}\frac{x^2}{2!} + \overline{(Mk^3)}\frac{x^3}{3!} - \cdots \qquad [16]$$

In [16] the values of the coefficients are not simply functions of the average parameters, $\overline{M}$ and $\bar{k}$, but rather averages of the products, Mk, Mk^2, etc., and therefore the averaging process is not legitimate, as has been indicated by Sidman for this function. It will be apparent that the failure of the exponential growth function to satisfy the criterion results from the fact that $\bar{y}$ is dependent not upon the parameters, as such, but upon a variety of products of the parameters; and the mean of a series of products is not necessarily the same as the product of the means. Since the average curve depends upon these individual products, no inferences can be made about the nature of the individual functions from the average curve without knowledge of these individual products. Furthermore, if we knew enough about the individual functions to ascertain these individual products, the average curve would be quite gratuitous.

The General
and the Aggregate

The failure to distinguish between general-type and aggregate-type propositions is at the root of a considerable amount of confusion that currently prevails in psychology. There are important differences in the research methods appropriate to these two types of propositions. The use of methods appropriate to one type in the establishment and confirmation of the other leads to error. A concrete instance of the failure to make this distinction properly has been dealt with (see pages 30–33). In the following discussion we

34

are concerned primarily with what a proposition is presumably about, and secondarily with the truth of a proposition.

The distinction may be put as follows: A general-type proposition asserts something presumably true of each and every member of a designable class. An aggregate-type proposition asserts something presumably true of the class considered as an aggregate.

The following exemplify general-type propositions: "The greater the physical difference between the standard and comparison stimuli, the fewer are the erroneous judgments which the subject makes"; "Habit strength increases as an exponential growth function of the number of trials"; and "An intense emotional conflict is the necessary basis for neurotic behavior."

The following exemplify aggregate-type propositions: "Ten per cent of the mothers in the study had IQ's above 110"; "The difference between the means is significant at the 5 per cent level of significance"; and "The correlatiton between Test A and Test B is .80."

Whereas general-type propositions require a class of a plurality of members only for validation, aggregate-type propositions require a class of a plurality of members that they be sensible.

If we restrict the application of analysis of variance to those instances in which the measure being analyzed is drawn on a one-score-one-organism basis, thereby providing for the possibility of an unqualified satisfaction of the requirement of independence of observations, then the aggregate nature of propositions which emerge from the use of this and allied techniques is evident. The analysis of variance is essentially a technique for making comparisons among scores. For any given set of scores the total sum of squares, regardless of all further partitioning, is essentially a function of the differences between members of each pair of scores. This is evident from the following formula:[1]

[1] This formula is the expansion of

$$\sum_{i=1}^{u} (X_i - \bar{X})^2 = \sum_{i=1}^{n} \left(\frac{i-1}{i}\right) \left(\frac{\sum_{z=1}^{i} X_z - iX_i}{i-1}\right)^2.$$

35

$$\sum_{i=1}^{n} (X_i - \bar{X})^2 = \frac{1}{2} \left[\frac{(X_1 - X_2)}{1} \right]^2 + \frac{2}{3} \left[\frac{(X_1 - X_3) + (X_2 - X_3)}{2} \right]^2$$
$$+ \cdots + \frac{n-1}{n} \left[\frac{(X_1 - X_n) + \cdots + (X_{n-1} - X_n)}{n-1} \right]^2$$

Both types of propositions may be expressions of variation and hence both are subject to mathematical formulation. However, unless buttressed with considerable qualification, statistical propositions, which are special instances of mathematical propositions, are aggregate-type propositions.

The cogency of the distinction between the two types of propositions is revealed by the different role that is played in connection with them of the "next" case. The "next" case presents a fundamental threat to the validity of a general-type proposition. General-type propositions are thus critically testable, since they are jeopardized by each new instance. If a general-type proposition fails to be confirmed by the observation of a member of the class to which the proposition presumably applies, then either the proposition must be rejected or the class must be more closely delimited. The "next" case, for the aggregate-type proposition, simply increases the "power" of the test, the likelihood of rejecting the null hypothesis, if the sttudy is properly conducted with respect to randomness, etc.

The distinction between the two types of propositions does not preclude the possibility of using one type of proposition as a basis for inference with respect to the other type. However, this is quite different from the syncretic substitution of inappropriate research methods. Statistical inference, as usually conceived, is not a way of making inferences about one type of proposition from the other. It is, rather, a way of making inferences about the population-aggregate from the study of the sample-aggregate.

Its proof is based on the identity:

$$\sum_{i=1}^{m} (X_i - \bar{X}_m)^2 - \sum_{=1}^{m-1} (X_i - \bar{X}_{m-1})^2 = \frac{m-1}{m} \left(\frac{\sum_{i=1}^{m} X_i - mXm}{m-1} \right)^2.$$

4

The Mystery-Mastery
Complex in
Contemporary Psychology

I believe that the mystery-mastery complex is one of the major forces interfering with our understanding of the nature of human personality, and that for this reason it deserves attention. The complex of which I speak consists in the simultaneous pursuit of two objectives: to keep the nature of human personality from being understood, to preserve it under a cloak of mystery; and to master, or predict and control, the behavior of human beings. Put in this way, it is clear that the two objectives—to keep the nature of the psyche a mystery and master human behavior—are incompatible with each other.

The objective of maintaining the psyche in a shroud of mystery can be seen as being rooted both in the nature of the psyche itself, and within certain cultural forces which have tended to reinforce this tendency within the psyche. In the microcosm of the clinical situation this has been identified as repression, where the individual hides his own nature from himself, and resistance, where the individual hides his nature from the psychoanalyst. One of the important things we have learned from the research of the psychoanalysts is that these two forms of mystery-keeping are intimately intertwined with each other. The uses of mystery have been amply documented in the psychoanalytic literature, in which mystery has been recognized as a primary defense against insult or injury from within or without.

Perhaps less profound but equally important is the role of mystery, or better, secrecy in all interpersonal relations. In the social spheres one of the major defenses that the individual has, even if it does not entail self-deception as in the case of the individuals involved in the clinical situation, is the keeping of secrets—the secret of his state of affairs, or the secrets of his intentions. We all recognize that in the social, political, economic, and military spheres knowledge of the secrets of others gives one the "advantage," and that discretion, in the sense of revealing only what one wishes to reveal, is valuable both in protecting ourselves from others and in manipulating others. Whereas mystery is the protection against the mastery impulse of others, it is also an objective which must be suspended for thoroughgoing mastery. Because in our total society we would be both masters and yet unmastered, we walk the complicated path of pursuing both the objectives of mystery and mastery.

Certain features of the growth of modern society, in particular the growth of urbanization and industrialization of the nineteenth and twentieth centuries, have worked to encourage the mystery-mastery complex. An outstanding characteristic of these modern developments has been the bringing together into significant interactions persons who were strangers. It is precisely in the interaction among strangers that both mystery and mastery become significant, the former being the initial condition, the latter the issue among strangers. Ideologically and culturally it was the Protestant ethic, as Max Weber described it (Weber, 1958), which entered as a major support to the mystery-mastery complex. Weber has shown that it was a significant feature in the development of the contemporary world, and David McClelland (1961) has piled up great quantities of data to show its working in the society of today. The Protestant ethic was associated with an intense psychological separation of individual from individual. It had a theology which suggested that the thoughts, feelings, and wishes of each individual were a matter between himself and God alone, and not a matter for another man to concern himself with. It tended to substitute formal and contractual forms of relationship for intimate interpsychic contact. A too great interest in the inner life of another person not only exceeded the bounds of formal relationship, but was also a reminder of the odious Confessional of the Catholic Church. At the same time the Protestant ethic was associated with a vaulting thrust to master the world through industry and through science.[1]

Psychology emerged in the modern world simultaneously with the growth of modern industrialization and urbanization; and this context can help us to understand the developments within our discipline. Thus, for example, this context helps us to understand the emergence on the American scene of its two major psychologies, behaviorism and psychoanalysis. Behaviorism fully deferred to the ideology by dramatically announcing its lack of interest in the psyche, thus insuring that the psyche would remain shrouded in mystery on the assumption that it did not exist, or that it was not subject to scientific investigation. At the same time it committed itself to the mastery objective by announcing that "prediction and control" were its ends. Psychoanalysis, on the other hand, ruthlessly violated the taboo on the mystery of the psyche. Its career in the United States has been very vigorous, but also kind of underworldly. Its major supporters have been the rebels against the alienation associated with modern urban-industrial society, the pockets of re-

[1] Cf. Merton (1936), who shows the intimate relationship between the Protestant ethic and science.

39

sistance among artists, writers, and some intellectuals. Even today, psychoanalysis has not been given much official recognition in the academic institutions. It has received its principal publicity from the popular press and the arts—and the use of psychoanalysis in therapy has been a highly guarded enterprise, and not that widespread. It might be pointed out parenthetically that Rogerian psychotherapy, which has been much more palatable than psychoanalysis in many respects, dealt gingerly with the unveiling of the mystery of the psyche, and has compensated for its small degree of violating the taboo on mystery by simultaneously denouncing the mastery objective, calling itself "nondirective."

It was difficult for psychology, in the simple etymological sense of the term as the study of the psyche, to develop in the larger mystery-mastery context of our society. The great uneasiness, which has been characteristic of psychology, about its status among the disciplines can be understood as rooted in the awkwardness of fit between its intrinsic objective of understanding the psyche and the mystery-mastery complex. The major point of this paper is that the art of research became to a considerable extent the art of finding a way between the taboo on penetrating the mystery of psychological functioning and the at least symbolic fulfillment of the mastery objective. In order to clarify this let us consider five different but related features which characterize much of the contemporary research enterprise. Each one of these features manages to help the psychologist in living within the mystery-mastery paradox by somehow appearing to serve both of the objectives:

1. The scientist-subject distinction.

2. The definition of psychology as the study of behavior.

3. The choice of lower animals, particularly domesticated animals, as subjects-of-choice in research.

4. The specification of the aim of research as the discovery of "laws."

5. The cultural norm that research consists of the testing of preconceived hypotheses.

I must at this point say that I do not mean to suggest anything so foolish or dogmatic as that these features cannot or have not served to increase our understanding. I in no way wish to disparage the excellent research which has been going on for what is now almost a century. However, I would suggest that a good deal of the understanding which we have won has been through processes going beyond those suggested by these five features. It is perhaps because psychologists are sensible people in addition to their being possessed of certain methodological tenets that our understanding has been enhanced. It is when psychologists allow themselves to go beyond the scientist-subject distinction, beyond the definition of psychology purely as behavior, beyond lower animals, beyond the presumptive regularities of the laws, and beyond the restriction of research to the testing of hypotheses that discoveries concerning the nature of and functioning of the human psyche have been revealed. If these features in some way constitute the "scientific superego" of psychologists, as I think they often do, then it is in the violation or circumvention of this scientific superego that our total investigatory enterprise has been advanced.

Let me comment briefly on each of these features, and try to point out the way in which they attempt to serve both mystery and mastery:

1. The scientist-subject distinction is a euphemism for manipulator-manipulated in many research situations. Insofar as the methodological literature on this distinction allows for the existence of the psyche at all, it confounds the issue by presuming at least two different kinds of psyche. It ascribes autonomy, methodicalness, and rationality—which are, by the way, characteristics of Weber's Protestant capitalist—to the one, but rarely to the other. In the methodological literature this is formulated in terms of two "languages," one that the scientist uses in discussing the phenomena, and one which is a "protocol language" used by subjects. If, for example, one tries to understand the nature of the research enterprise by bringing to bear findings concerning the growth of thought, the methodological "sophisticate" cries out "genetic fallacy!" as though he were an umpire yelling "foul!" The concept of such two languages characteristically makes the scientist and the subject

strangers to each other—a strangeness which, as we have already said, is the underlying condition of the mystery-mastery complex in the first place. In the experimental situation the scientist is the master, the subject the one who is mastered. By the studied ignorance of the meaning of the subject's protocol language the scientist guarantees that he will not enter upon the psyche of the subject. Not that the scientist will not learn something about the subject's protocol language; but he will not allow himself to think what the subject's protocol language is really about.

2. The definition of psychology as the study of behavior is perhaps the outstanding device by which the two objectives of mystery of the psyche and mastery are served. It rules out the psyche by fiat, and thus guarantees that it is not a fit area for investigation. At the same time it takes as its central concern what the mastery objective is most critically interested in, the behavior of the other person. Being able to master another person means to master his behavior, to make him act in accordance with the master's wishes.

3. The use of animals as subjects-of-choice in much investigation is particularly interesting from this point of view. The muteness of animals insures that they will not complicate the situation with reports on their thoughts or feelings or wishes. An additional factor is that psychologists have tended to choose domestic animals. Domestic animals are animals which are already given to and selected and bred for docility and tractability, which is to say that they are easily mastered. The work of the ethologists, of course, represents a significant deviation from this and should be cited to demonstrate that domesticity of animals is not a prerequisite for their being useful in psychological research.

4. The notion that the aim of psychology is the discovery of laws can be illuminated by an observation which was made by a student of Machiavelli. In a book called *The Statecraft of Machiavelli* Herbert Butterfield (1940) says that the thrust to control other people entails the assumption of an unchanging nature of those who are to be controlled. As has been pointed out by Max Planck (1937), the eminent physicist, and others, such control is

also premised on the assumption that those who are being controlled are ignorant of the presumptive regularities that the controller is aware of. This is not the place to enter into a discussion of the various problems associated with the notion of "law." Yet it should be pointed out that, although empirical data have often compromised the notion, it has had a remarkable stubbornness, a stubbornness even greater among psychologists than physicists. The stubbornness of the notion inheres, we believe, in the way in which it appears to serve the two objectives of mystery and mastery. The service of the mastery objective is patent. The mystery is preserved by formulating these laws on the basis of research in which the information concerning the presumptive regularities are concealed from the subjects, and by never allowing a theoretical place for the knowledge of these regularities as factors in human functioning. One of the most ubiquitous fears of investigators is that the human subjects will not be "naive," that they might be aware of the nature of the phenomenon under investigation. Few things can mess up research as can the subject having read the literature relevant to the study. Put another way we can say that there is a fact concerning human functioning that is rarely taken into account: that human beings make use of their generalizations concerning the nature of human functioning in their functioning. This is one of the factors involved in the mystery of the psyche which is systematically excluded in the search for laws.

5. I would like to preface what I have to say about the notion of research as the testing of preconceived hypotheses with the observation that there are, in the normal educational career of the contemporary psychologist, two important moments. The first, which characteristically takes place in his first course in psychology, is when he learns that he should not be interested in mind. Frequently this lesson is learned from a dialogue that the instructor has with the class in the early days of the term. The instructor asks the class what they think psychology is. Before long some student who is proud to be able to show off his primitive knowledge of Greek says that it is the study of the mind. This is the opening that the instructor has been waiting for: "O.K.! What is mind?" The

answers he gets are easily demolished, and then the students are properly prepared. Since we "obviously" do not know what we are talking about when we use the word "mind," why do we not just forget about it, and go on with the study of psychology! The latter consists in large part in bringing the students around to accepting the five features I have outlined. The fact of the matter is that every science has its ultimate mystery. In biology, the ultimate mystery is life; in physics, it is the nature of light; in chemistry, the nature of matter. No biologist would maintain that it would be necessary for him to define life before he could go on to investigate biological phenomena. In psychology, of course, the ultimate mystery is mind; and the ultimate mysteriousness of mind should not be used as an excuse to be mindless about psychological phenomena.

The second important moment comes early in the psychologist's graduate career when he learns that research consists of the testing of hypotheses. Curiosity, interest in the phenomena, or even the complex psychodynamics associated with the getting of hypotheses are brushed aside or, at best, are regarded as "private processes," about which the least said the better. What the student desperately needs is a testable hypothesis, and it is perfectly all right to beg one, borrow one, steal one. What testability in fact consists of is the enumeration of a set of alternatives. The function of the data-collecting process is simply to choose among the alternatives which have been previously conceived of. A good deal of the burden has fallen on "significant" or "not significant," a difference which, as we are painfully becoming aware, is itself not that significant. Again, I must qualify. There is nothing intrinsically wrong with testing hypotheses. It is an important part of the total investigatory enterprise. What I do wish to point out, however, is that by the time the investigatory enterprise has reached the stage of testing hypotheses, most of the important work, if there has been any, has already been done. One is tempted to think that psychologists are often like children playing cowboys. When children play cowboys they emulate them in everything but their main work, which is taking care of cows. The main work of the scientist is

44

thinking and making discoveries of what was not thought of beforehand. Psychologists often attempt to "play scientist" by avoiding the main work.

The elevation of the hypothesis-testing stage to the point where it is conceived of as practically the entire investigatory enterprise is in the service of the mystery-mastery complex. The preconception of the alternatives, and the disciplined limitation of the investigation to them, cuts out the possibility of surprise, the learning of something which was not thought of beforehand. (We might point out parenthetically that a good deal of the bickering which has been going on in the literature concerning the use of one-tailed or two-tailed tests hangs precisely on the question as to whether the alternative involving the one-tailed test was thought of before or after the time when the data were collected. See pp. 17–19 above.) The obligation to preconceive the alternatives tends to preserve the mystery of the psyche, by eliminating what is not "proper." To put this in another way, our ideal of research is more in terms of confirmation than discovery. The mastery objective is served by selection of preconceived alternatives which fulfill it and elimination of others. This part of the process is hardly acknowledged, hardly evaluated, and hardly the object of critical thought. It is, so to speak, "free"; and insofar as it is free it becomes the likely locus for the operation of the psychological and cultural factors which bind us and of which we are unaware. For, as we have learned from the various investigations concerning the nature of free responses in projective testing and the like, whatever is free is whatever is the result of our deepest predilections. To put this yet another way, our deep penchant for "control" of variables in our research enterprise is the façade for our penchant for mastery, not only of the variables in the limited sense in which we use this term, but in the larger sense of the control of the behavior of others. In the interests of control in research, we select such sets of alternatives which promise the greatest degree of control of the behavior of those whom we study.

The dynamic associated with the two objectives of mystery and mastery is such that they tend to reinforce each other in spite of the contradiction between them. If the psyche is to be maintained as a mystery, then one is pressed into mastery by default. If one moves to uncover the mystery of the psyche in a condition of interpersonal alienation, then there is an intensification of mystery as a defense. Our clinical experience has made us aware of the way in which an amalgam of mutually reinforcing contradictions can inhibit the psychological growth of the individual. The mystery-mastery complex is the neurotic core of the contemporary psychological research enterprise. This complex of mystery and mastery may not, perhaps, inhibit the multiplication of research papers (although I am sure that it even does this for some psychologists) as a kind of "repetition compulsion," but it does inhibit the genuine growth of our collective understanding of the nature of human functioning. For understanding necessarily entails the suspension of the taboo on mystery.

But, one may ask, why, if this mystery-mastery complex of which I have been speaking appears to keep at least some of us in motion, should we abandon it? In order to answer this question we need to move to considerations concerning the relationship of psychology to the society at large. I have already indicated that the mystery-mastery complex in psychology is a reflection of the same complex in the larger society, that it is an expression within our science of the same factors which were associated with the development of urbanization and industrialization, that is, with the making of the modern world.

My answer to this question hinges on the fact that the world is changing, and changing in such a way that psychology has a new and important place in it. Insofar as psychology still maintains the mystery-mastery complex it is participating in the phenomenon of "cultural lag." The mystery-mastery complex has been an important feature in the total development of the society to the present point, but it is rapidly becoming archaic in terms of the changes which are taking place in the larger society itself. The crises of our contemporary society—the cold war, the possibility of nuclear warfare, the problems of educating masses of people, the problems of the interaction of alien cultures, the problems of the underdeveloped nations—all call for an understanding by human beings of each other at a considerably higher level than ever before; and neither mystery nor mastery is a sensible objective anymore.

It may be very bold to attempt to characterize our total society in a few sentences. Yet one can reasonably say that there are two major commitments to which we have come in the last few decades. First, there is the commitment of men to live with each other in highly complex interrelationships; and the network of interrelationships continues to enlarge so that before long every person alive on the face of the earth will in some way be related to every other person. Second, there is the commitment of mankind to manage its own affairs. We no longer trust to fate, destiny, "the invisible hand of God" (as Adam Smith put it), unguided natural law, or some single authoritarian "master." It is man in general who is to manage things. These two commitments tend to make the two objectives of mystery and mastery archaic. We need to understand our own psyches and the psyches of others; we need to stop being strangers to each other. And the mastery of man over man is increasingly intolerable, untolerated, and futile.

For several centuries the physical scientist has been important in connection with the major social developments. It is from the knowledge gleaned by the physical scientist that great cities and factories were made possible. I believe that what the physical scientists have been to the world of the past, the social scientists will be to the world of the future. As the physical scientists have made it possible to modify the world to increase its habitability, the social scientists will serve the two commitments I have mentioned.

Yet it would be wrong for the psychologist to enter upon the larger scene in precisely the social role of the physical scientist. The knowledge of the physical scientist becomes socially significant as it is mediated, applied, and used in design of processes and equipment. His knowledge of heat, or electricity, or mechanics becomes significant as it is used in making devices of which we avail ourselves without necessarily understanding the nature of heat or electricity or mechanics. The physical scientist was able to turn his knowledge into use without teaching us what he knew. But the

47

value of the understanding of human functioning does not inhere in its application in the usual sense, but in its possession. This is one of the most significant results of the clinical enterprise. In order to help a person who is in psychological difficulties we work to enhance his understanding of himself and of his relationships to others. If we think in terms of traditional social roles, then the significant place in society of the psychologist will be more that of teacher than expert or technician. For the psychologist to play a useful social role, it is important that he work to uncover the mystery of the psyche and teach people to understand themselves and each other. In this way they can be helped to live with each other and manage their affairs effectively.

The psychologist is not intrinsically different from other people. All people seek to understand themselves and others in the course of their lives; and all people continually attempt to bring to bear such generalizations in the management of their lives. The special character of the psychologist inheres only in the intensity and systematic nature of his search. The special responsibility that he has is to teach what he learns.

Not too long ago a very able graduate student told me that he had decided to leave school, and that he no longer wanted to be a psychologist. I was very much taken aback by this. He was bright, doing well, and receiving a good stipend. In the course of conversation he made one remark which spoke of his deep feelings about psychology. He told me that he did not want to become a "hollow man" and that he was afraid that if he stayed he would become one. As he spoke I recalled a discussion we had had about the concept of the "empty organism," and it occurred to me that this may well be a metaphorical projection of the state into which we were trying to discipline our young psychologists. For the mystery-mastery complex forces a conception of hollowness upon both scientist and subject as it tries to keep them apart.

In this discussion I have presumed one of my conclusions: that the scientist-subject distinction is a reflection of the mystery-mastery complex, and that the mystery-mastery complex needs to be abandoned in favor of understanding. I would like to think that

48

the position that I am advancing is in line with the injunction for psychology to become more operationistic. I do not mean this term in the sense in which it is characteristically used by psychologists, but rather in its original sense that we need to be more aware of the factors associated with the knowledge-getting processes. We need to become much more aware of the operation of psychological and cultural factors in our own research operations, for they largely constitute the operations of our investigatory work. What we ordinarily call methodology needs to be expanded to include the culture and psychology of psychologists. By allowing this to happen we can both avoid becoming hollow men and relate more meaningfully to the culture at large.

Learning
and the
Scientific Enterprise

Whoever has given thought to the problems inherent in current views of learning phenomena might well wonder whether it is appropriate possibly to confound the issues by drawing attention to the fact that the scientific enterprise itself is a learning enterprise. In a sense, this point is banal. In another sense, it is not; for it has been largely ignored and systematically banished by some theorists (Bergmann and Spence, 1944).

Skinner (1950) has raised the question, "Are theories of

learning necessary?" and has answered it in the negative. He has indicated that we can do better and faster without the types of learning theories which are currently available. In effect, what Skinner has done is to raise the controversy between empiricism and rationalism. But in doing so, Skinner also advances, by implication, a view concerning the nature of human learning. In effect, what Skinner is saying is that the attitude of empiricism is more conducive to efficient learning than is the attitude of rationalism. He makes an assertion about the role of attitude in human learning. This he does by advocating that the scientist shall concern himself primarily with the collection of data rather than the construction of elaborate theoretical systems. To quote him directly:

> An adequate impetus is supplied by the inclination to obtain data showing orderly changes characteristic of the learning process. An acceptable scientific program is to collect data of this sort and to relate them to manipulable variables, selected for study through a common sense exploration of the field.

In advocating one "scientific" approach rather than another, one must necessarily be presupposing a hypothesis concerning the nature of human learning. The scientific enterprise is a learning enterprise. Thus any point of view which asserts what is good scientific method presupposes a theory of human learning. The thesis of this essay is that if we were carefully to examine our views concerning the nature of the scientific enterprise, we might be in an excellent position to advance our understanding of the processes of human learning. In the same way that we were able to advance our understanding about the nature of human personality by the study of extremes, so might we be able to advance our understanding of the learning process by the study of an extreme in human learning, namely, the learning of the scientist.

There is a point of view in the field of psychology which sets up a "methodological" distinction between the scientist and the subject (Bergmann and Spence, 1944). "Methodologically" it differentiates between the man in his functioning as a scientist and in his functioning as a human being. This distinction is both unfortunate and unreal. Its maintenance closes off from our view one of the richest sources of information about human learning that we have. The distinction makes it impossible, in principle, if not in practice, to study the learning of the scientist in his learning operations. In advocating this distinction Bergmann and Spence (1944) write:

> In the schema outlined by the scientific empiricist the experiences of the observing scientist do indeed have a privileged, even unique, position. If pressed too far and without the necessary epistemological sophistication, this account of the scientist's position can very easily lead to a metaphysical thesis of the solipsistic type.

The nature of this "epistemological sophistication" is given to us by these writers as follows:

> . . . the empiristic scientist should realize that his behavior, symbolic or otherwise, does not lie on the same methodological level as the responses of his subjects.

Whatever "methodological" distinctions we may attempt to draw, we cannot escape from the brute fact that the scientist's "behavior, symbolic or otherwise" is behavior, and is, more particularly, learning behavior. We are hardly convinced that the acceptance of what the scientist does as behavior will lead us to solipsism, with the exception of one aspect of the solipsist position. The aspect of solipsism to which we refer is its emphasis on the creative character of learning, a feature indicated by Tolman (1934), who is hardly a solipsist. Indeed, the methodological distinction preserves rather than justifies a "privileged . . . unique position" for the experiences of the scientist. Thereby it grants creativity to the scientist, but denies it to the subject.

Not only does this distinction between scientist and subject cut off the opportunity for the examination of the scientific enterprise as an example of learning, but also tends to lead us into error in our investigations. To demonstrate this latter point, let us examine the notion that the stimulus is an independent variable. We take the notion of the stimulus as an example to point out one type of error that the "methodological" distinction can foster; and also we offer the analysis of the stimulus notion as an example of the type of analysis of the scientific enterprise which is being advocated.

The stimulus as an independent variable is a notion quite taken for granted by the "scientific empiricist." Spence (1944) characterizes stimulus variables as follows:

> S-variables: measurements of physical and social environmental factors and conditions (present and past) under which the responses of organisms occur. These are sometimes referred to as the independent, manipulable variables.

The questions of whether the word "variable" applies, or the word "independent" applies, are not generally raised. Certainly the recent work on the effect of personality and attitude on perception can well lead us to ask whether we really know what we mean by a stimulus. A recognition of the difficulty inherent in this matter of perception is manifested in the effort to reconcile the lack of independence of the stimulus with Hullian theory (Berlyne, 1951).

What do we mean by a variable? Let us consider two items, the status of which as variables would hardly be challenged, say, length and color. By virtue of what may these be considered to be variables? First, that they vary, that is, that there are two or more lengths and that there are two or more colors. Second, that the designated categories of the variables shall be mutually exclusive, that is, if something be of one length, it not be of another length, and if something be of one color, it not be of another color. What distinguishes one variable from another is that the criterion of mutual exclusiveness does not apply, that is, if something be of one color it may be of any length, and if something be of one length

53

it may be of any color. Thus we arrive at a definition of a variable:

A variable is a set of two or more categories such that, if any object or event be a member of one of those categories, it may not be a member of any other of those categories.

Let us consider some of the implications of this definition for the notion of a stimulus variable. Let us avoid getting into the metaphysical question by simply saying that the real world is what it is, without any further elaboration. However, whatever the nature of the real world may be, and without in any way denying the existence of the real world, the constitution[1] of the variable as a variable is the work, or invention, or creation, of the scientist. Variables, whatever they may be *in re,* do not exist there as variables. For variables are, by definition, sets of categories; and categories are the result of someone's delineation, abstraction, and identification.

By virtue of these considerations, if it were not so tedious, it would be more appropriate to talk of variables-as-constituted-by-the-scientist, rather than simply of variables. The refinement introduced by this distinction is less important in the physical sciences, since it would be rather meaningless to talk of variables-as-constituted-by-the-subject. Even in the physical sciences, following the notions of Bridgman (1938), the distinction is appropriate. However, this distinction is extremely important in the psychology of learning, for here we have the constitution of variables by both the experimenter and the subject.

To clarify this point, let us consider a more or less typical experimental situation in the psychology of learning. Consider a Skinner box, with a lever, the depression of which by the animal results in the delivery of a food pellet. The animal is placed in the box. Is there any constitution of the stimulus variable on the part of the animal? Not at the outset of the experiment. However, the lever is constituted at the outset of the experiment as a stimulus variable by the experimenter. (The categories of the variable in

---

[1] We borrow this word from Dewey's *The reflex arc concept in psychology* (1896). Much of what is being said here is based on our interpretation of some of the notions in Dewey's paper.

this case are presence or absence of the lever.) It is delineated from the remainder of the environment, the property of leverness has been abstracted, and it is identified as a lever the depression of which leads to the delivery of a food pellet, by the experimenter, at the outset of the experiment.

As "learning" takes place or proceeds, the animal comes to depress the lever with greater and greater regularity. The animal, it may be said, comes to learn what's what. We prefer "what's what" to the Tolmanian "what leads to what" since the former, to us, seems to include the delineation and the abstraction more than the latter does. The animal delineates the lever from the remainder of the environment, avails itself of its leverness, and identifies it as leading to food. Essentially, what takes place in this type of experimental situation is that the animal comes, after the learning process, to constitute the stimulus variable in much the same way as the experimenter did at the outset of the experiment.

The usual experimental learning situation is a teaching situation, more particularly, than a learning situation. The success of the learning is indicated by the degree to which the animal seems to have constituted the stimulus variable as the experimenter has constituted the stimulus variable. The latter is exactly what is meant by the learning criterion in most experiments in the psychology of learning.

The "methodological" distinction between scientist and subject prevents us from seeing that the psychological processes of the experimenter are an integral part of the nature of the experimental situation. Furthermore it leads us into the error of generalizing from such experimental situations to learning in general, when actually it is the special case of learning which we might call teaching or communication. "Methodologically" it removes the experimenter from the "data" when actually his psychological processes are "data" too; and necessary data for the understanding of the nature of the experimental situation.

We have concerned ourselves with the variable aspect of the stimulus variable. Let us now turn our attention to the question of the independence of the stimulus variable. What is generally meant by the independence of the stimulus is that it is independent of the response. The paradigm is that the response is dependent on the stimulus, but the stimulus is independent of the response. The formulation of this paradigm is

$$R = f(S).$$

But even here, the question is begged. For, in the explanation of what a stimulus variable is, the expression "under which the responses of organisms occur" (Spence, 1944) is used. The stimulus does not exist as a stimulus except by virtue of the responses of the organism. The delineation, abstraction, and identification of the stimulus is the response.

The only kind of independence the stimulus variable can have is a spurious one. The delineation, abstraction, and identification of the stimulus variable by the experimenter is independent of the delineation, abstraction, and identification of the stimulus variable by the subject. But in the subject himself there is no such independence.

The operationist argument to the effect that our knowledge is contingent upon the operations we engage in in obtaining this knowledge can well be leveled against the conception that the stimulus variable is independent of the response. For we cannot even identify the stimulus properly without taking account of the responses of the organism. If this is true, we can hardly talk of the independence of the stimulus variable.

Again, we might point out that the fallacy of considering the stimulus variable as independent may be viewed as stemming from the "methodological" distincttion between scientist and subject. It can be said that, by virtue of not taking account of his psychological processes, the investigator is led into a position where he "projects" his prior constitution of the stimulus into the organism that is the subject in the experiment.

The point which has been made above, that it is inappropriate to talk of the independent stimulus variable, has, interestingly enough, been made in current discussions of the scientific method by some of the same persons who talk of the independent stimulus variable. The point is an essential one of operationism. It has, however, not been brought to bear as an insight concerning learning. Thus, for example, Bridgman (1938) has given priority, not to the stimulus, but to the response. Basic to scientific learning is not the stimulus, but the operations of the scientist. Similarly, Stevens (1939), accepting the priority of the operation, goes on further to specify the nature of the operation as being discrimination, a response. Bergmann and Spence (1941), aside from their particular views on the psychology of learning proper, have emphasized the response feature of the scientist's learning, in their emphasis on theory construction and theory creation. In spite of their avowed point of view concerning the distinction between scientist and subject, they still permit themselves to say:

> Historically and *psychologically*, then, the *creation* of helpful concepts is a very essential part of a scientific achievement [our italics].

and:

> Actually much of what is usually called theorizing in empirical science consists . . . in the *creation* of these organizing empirical constructs . . . [our italics].

In these writings we find not only a stress upon the response priority in the learning situation, but also the creative aspects which are involved in learning. We have here a stress upon a feature of human learning which is rarely mentioned in the works on the psychology of learning proper. It is of more than parenthetical interest that Hull's *Principles of Behavior* (1943), an effort in human learning, is certainly worthy of the adjective "creative."

57

♣ ♣ ♣ ♣ ♣ ♣ *6*

Learning and the
Principle of
Inverse Probability

The basic idea that has guided the theoretical explorations contained in this chapter is that science is a way of learning. This thesis and some of its implications have been discussed in the preceding essay. Here the attempt is made to gain an understanding of the nature of the learning process through the examination of one particular formulation of the nature of the scientific method, the principle of inverse probability. In brief, this principle formulates the effect of a confirmation on the probability of a theory. In thus formulating one important aspect of the scientific method, it should tell us something of the psychology of learning.

In a sense, what follows can be considered to be the elaboration of Hull's "hidden" theory of learning; for Hull has not one but two theories of learning. One of these is what is generally understood to be Hull's theory; the other is contained in his discussions on method, particularly the introductory sections of Hull (1943) and Hull *et al.* (1940), and can be called the "hypothetico-deductive theory of learning." In this latter, a theory of how the scientist learns, the three major concepts are theory, observation, and probability. Probability is what characterizes the relation between theory and observation. Thus, on the grounds of certain observations, a theory is said to have such and such a probability. On the grounds of a given theory, a predicted observation has such and such a probability of occurring. When a predicted observation is verified, the probability of the theory goes up. When a predicted observation fails to be verified, the probability of the theory goes down.

This "hidden" theory of learning is more of a cognitive than an S-R theory. It points almost directly to the principle of inverse probability.

According to Jeffries (1931), the principle of inverse probability "is to the theory of probability what Pythagoras's theorem is to geometry." Although the principle is one of the most critical bones of contention among probability theorists, it is mathematically sound. This is attested to by Uspensky (1937), who says "Bayes' formula, and other conclusions derived from it, are necessary consequences of fundamental concepts and theorems of the theory of probability. Once we admit these fundamentals, we must admit Bayes' formula and all that follows from it." The major question is its applicability.

Probability theorists fall into two general categories: frequency theorists and nonfrequency theorists.[1] The frequency theo-

---

[1] Nagel (1947) has summarized the controversy. Nagel himself accepts the frequency point of view and presents a rather weak case for the nonfrequency point of view. A balanced picture of the situation can be had

rist insists on an "objective" definition of probability in terms of relative frequency. The nonfrequency theorist considers probability to be a kind of rating scale of credence. Probability is, according to the nonfrequency theorist, "The state of mind with respect to an assertion, a coming event, or any other matter on which absolute knowledge does not exist" (De Morgan, 1849). The basic syntactical unit for the nonfrequency theorist is $P(g/h)$,[2] the probability of g on the grounds of h. If g necessarily follows from h, as in deduction, then $P(g/h) = 1$. If g is impossible on the data h, then $P(g/h) = 0$.

On the philosophical level no position is taken on this controversy here. Acceptance of the principle is only on the grounds of its cogency to what it might mean for the psychology of learning.

The principle of inverse probability formulates the effect on the probability of a proposition g of the verification of a proposition x. Let us say that, on the basis of a previously acquired set of propositions h, a proposition g has the probability $P(g/h)$. Then, say, a proposition x is found to be true. What is the effect of finding x to be true on the probability of g? A root form[3] of the principle (Jeffries, 1931) provides us with the answer:

---

by reading Nagel on the controversy in general, supplemented with, perhaps, Keynes's (1948) presentation of the nonfrequency point of view.

[2] The symbol "/" should not be confused with this symbol used to indicate division. It does not indicate division as used here. It should be read "on" or "on the grounds of."

[3] This is immediately derivable from the theorem of compound probability. This theorem is:

$$P(ABC) = P(A)P(B/A)P(C/AB). \qquad (a)$$

We then have

$$P(hgx) = P(h)P(g/h)P(x/gh) \qquad (b)$$

and

$$P(hgx) = P(hxg) = P(h)P(x/h)P(g/hx) \qquad (c)$$

and

$$P(g/hx)P(x/h) = P(x/gh)P(g/h) \qquad (d)$$

and therefore

$$P(g/hx) = \frac{P(x/gh)}{P(x/h)} P(g/h). \qquad (e)$$

$$P(g/hx) = \frac{P(x/gh)}{P(x/h)} P(g/h). \qquad [1]$$

The probability that g is true on the grounds of h and x is equal to the probability that g is true on the grounds of h, multiplied by the ratio of the probability of x on g and h, to the probability of x on h (h alone).

Thus, if x stems equally well from g and h, as from h alone, the probability of g does not change. If, however, x follows from g and h with a probability greater than the probability of x on h alone, the probability of g increases. Similarly, if $P(x/gh)$ should be less than $P(x/h)$, the probability of $P(g/hx)$ is less than $P(g/h)$.

The nature of this formula will become evident if we make the following interpretations of g, h, and x: Let h be a set of propositions concerning data which have been collected; let g be a theory which has been developed to account for the data h; and let x be a proposition about a new datum which was not involved in the initial generation of g. The formula then expresses the most critical aspect of the hypothetico-deductive method, the effect of the confirmation of a deduction on the probability of the hypothesis that generated it. If x is found to be true, and x stems from the theory with a relatively high probability, then the probability of the theory is raised.

By appropriate algebraic manipulation,[4] formula [1] leads to

[4] From formula [1] we have

$$P(g/hx) = \frac{P(x/gh)}{P(x/h)} P(g/h) \qquad (a)$$

and therefore also

$$P(\bar{g}/hx) = \frac{P(x/\bar{g}h)}{P(x/h)} P(\bar{g}/h). \qquad (b)$$

By dividing (a) by (b), with

$$P(g/hx) + P(\bar{g}/hx) = 1,$$

with $P(g/h) + P(\bar{g}/h) = 1$, and letting

$$\frac{P(x/gh)}{P(x/\bar{g}h)} = R,$$

61

where P_n is the probability of g after the verification of x_n, and P_{n-1} is the probability of g prior to the verification of x_n, and R is the ratio of $P(x_n/\bar{g}h)$ to $P(x_n/\bar{g}h)$.   ($\bar{g} = $ not $-g$.)

An interpretation of g, h, and x as propositions concerning theory, old data, and new datum respectively has already been given. However, for the principle of inverse probability to have greater generality for the psychology of learning, we will widen the interpretation of these symbols. The crux of this wider interpretation is in the interpretation of x, with which we shall deal first.

Let x stand for the conditional proposition, "If Y, then X," where X is an observation on the part of the learning organism, and Y the conditions for the observation. By the verification of x, we mean the verification of this whole conditional proposition. Some examples may be helpful:

> *Instrumental conditioning:* $x = $ "If I press the bar, I will get a pellet of food."
> *Classical conditioning:* $x = $ "If the metronome ticks, meat powder will be injected into my mouth."
> *Problem solving:* $x = $ "If I do such and such, the obstacle will be overcome."
> *Prejudice:* $x = $ "If he is a Negro, then I will find him to be irresponsible."
> *Law:* $x = $ "If this body is immersed in this liquid, then it will be buoyed up by a force which is equal to the weight of the liquid it displaces."

With this as our understanding of the meaning of x, g is, then, whatever it is that generates x's. g is what is associated with the organism when we say that the organism has learned. It is the "what is learned" in the sense that we say that habits, attitudes,

---

we get

$$P(g/hx) = \frac{RP(g/h)}{RP(g/h) + [1 - P(g/h)]}. \tag{c}$$

$$P_n = \frac{RP_{n-1}}{RP_{n-1} + (1 - P_{n-1})}, \tag{2}$$

62

prejudices, skills, cognitions, hypotheses, etc., are learned. It should be emphasized that *g* is in no sense the overt behavior, but is, rather, the condition of the organism. The essential characteristic of *g* is that it can generate *x*'s.

The *h* is whatever led to the *g*. It consists of hereditary factors, maturational factors, and previous learnings.

"Reinforcement" may now be defined as the verification of *x*. We are now in a position to determine the amount of increase in the probability of *g* as a function of one reinforcement.

The amount of increase is given by the increment in the probability of *g*.

$$P_n - P_{n-1} = \frac{RP_{n-1}}{RP_{n-1} + (1 - P_{n-1})} - P_{n-1}. \qquad [3]$$

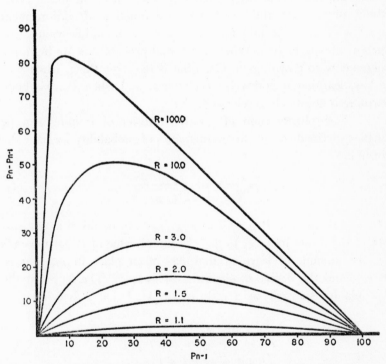

FIG. 1. The amount of increment, $P_n - P_{n-1}$, as a function of one "reinforcement," as a function of P_{n-1} and R

In Fig. 1, the values of the increment have been plotted for various values of R as a function of P_{n-1}. For any value of R which is greater than 1, the increment is low for both low and high values of P_{n-1}, and high for middle values of P_{n-1}.

Immediate empirical confirmation of the relationship indicated by this figure is to be found in phenomena of transfer of training. Roughly, where an individual approaches a "new" learning situation without already having very much to transfer to it, the initial learning of the new situation is slow, that is, when P_{n-1} is low, $P_n - P_{n-1}$ is low. If, however, P_{n-1} is a middle value, improvement is rapid; and if P_{n-1} is already high, there is little more room for improvement. The work of Harlow (1949) with respect to the learning of learning sets is a case in point. Translating his results into the terminology advanced here, where the initial probability of g is low, the increments as a function of reinforcement are low. Where the initial probabilities are of middle values, the increments are highest. Where the initial probabilities are high, the increments go down again. Or, what is the same thing, when P_{n-1} is low, learning is positively accelerated; and when P_{n-1} is high, learning is negatively accelerated.

The phenomenon of positive transfer of training can be further specified. From the mathematics of probability we have the formula:[5]

$$P(g_2) = P(g_1) \frac{P(g_2/g_1)}{P(g_1/g_2)}. \qquad [4]$$

The ratio of $P(g_2/g_1)$ to $P(g_1/g_2)$ can be taken as a measure of the similarity of g_2 to g_1. The initial value of $P(g_2)$ depends on the amount of learning that has taken place in g_1, that is, $P(g_1)$, and the degree of similarity of g_2 to g_1. The fact that the formula for similarity is a ratio of the kind that it is dramatizes

[5]
$$P(g_1 g_2) = P(g_1)P(g_2/g_1) \qquad \text{(a)}$$
$$P(g_1 g_2) = P(g_2 g_1) = P(g_2)P(g_1/g_2) \qquad \text{(b)}$$
$$P(g_2)P(g_1/g_2) = P(g_1)P(g_2/g_1) \qquad \text{(c)}$$
$$P(g_2) = P(g_1) \frac{P(g_2/g_1)}{P(g_1/g_2)}. \qquad \text{(d)}$$

the fact that similarity with respect to learning is a directional relationship, for example, the amount of positive transfer from French to Spanish is not necessarily the same as the amount of positive transfer from Spanish to French.

Although the initial value of $P(g_2)$ is dependent linearly on $P(g_1)$ and the similarity of g_2 to g_1, it should be emphasized that the *increment* in learning is not a linear function of $P(g_1)$. Rather, the relationship is that shown in Fig. 1.

The point of maximum learning for one reinforcement as a function of P_{n-1} varies with R. When R is high, the maximum is at low values of P_{n-1}. When R is low, the maximum is at higher values of P_{n-1}, although it is always at a value of P_{n-1} which is less than .50. Specifically, $P_n - P_{n-1}$ is maximal when[6]

$$P_{n-1} = \frac{\sqrt{R}-1}{R-1}. \qquad [5]$$

For the purposes of showing the progress in learning, formula [2] can be generalized to the form

$$P_n = \frac{R_1 R_2 \cdots R_n P_0}{R_1 R_3 \cdots R_n P_0 + (1 - P_0)}, \qquad [6]$$

where R_1 corresponds to x_1, etc., and P_0 is the probability of g prior to the verification of x_1.

For purposes of simplicity of exposition, let us assume that $R_1 = R_2 = \ldots = R_n$. The formula for the learning curve as a function of the number of reinforcements then becomes[7]

[6] This was obtained by differentiating $P_n - P_{n-1}$ with respect to P_{n-1}, setting the derivative equal to zero, and solving for P_{n-1}. It has a limit of .50 as R approaches 1, R being 1 or greater. When $R = 1$, the maximum is indeterminate.

[7] Dr. Nathan Shock has, with the assistance of Dr. Max Halperin, been able to demonstrate that this equation is essentially the same as one of his theoretically derived growth functions derived from the consideration of cell proliferation on the assumption that cells proliferate with equal and constant division times, and on the assumption that when the cells are

$$P_n = \frac{R^n P_0}{R^n P_0 + (1 - P_0)}. \qquad [7]$$

Figure 2 then shows various learning curves for various values of R. These curves run from S-shaped to growth-type curves to curves of sharp rise which may be called insight curves. When R is low, we have "trial-and-error" learning, which can be defined as learning which takes place when $P(x/gh)$ is not much larger than $P(x/\bar{g}h)$. Similarly, "insightful" learning takes place when $P(x/gh)$ is considerably larger than $P(x/\bar{g}h)$.[8]

---

brought together "each cell produces a substance that is harmful to every cell in the community including itself" (Shock, 1951). The equation is his equation (8). Equation (8) in his paper essentially is

$$N = \frac{\alpha}{1 + (\alpha - 1)e^{-\beta t}}.$$

The main difference between this equation and [7] is that it is continuous (t), while [7] is discrete (n). [7] can be written

$$P_n = \frac{1}{1 + \dfrac{1 - P_0}{P_0} R^{-n}},$$

by division of numerator and denominator by $R^n P_0$,

$$P_n = \frac{1}{1 + \dfrac{(1 - P_0)}{P_0} e^{-(\log R)n}},$$

by writing R^{-n} in exponential form. Thus, if one lets $(\log R) = \beta$, $n = t$,

$$\text{and} \quad \frac{1 - P_0}{P_0} = \alpha - 1,$$

the equation can be written $P_t = \dfrac{1}{1 + (\alpha - 1)e^{-\beta t}}$,

which differs only by a multiplicative constant. It must have been things like this that brought Leibniz to talk of preestablished harmony!

[8] Cf. Harlow (1949): "The very form of the learning curve changes as learning sets become more efficient. The form of the learning curve for the first eight discrimination problems appears S-shaped: it could be de-

By analogous reasoning, it is possible to derive the phenomenon of extinction. Extinction is the consequence of the verification of $\bar{x}$. The result on the probability of g of the verification of $\bar{x}_m$ is

$$P_m = \frac{P_{m-1}}{P_{m-1} + \bar{R}(1 - P_{m-1})}, \qquad [8]$$

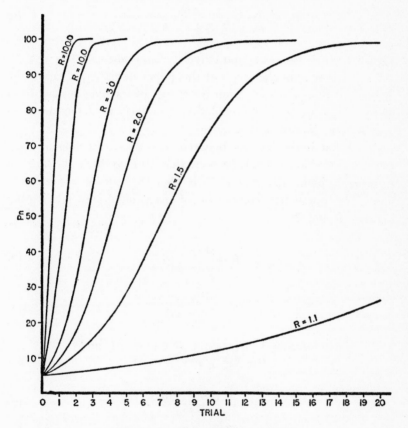

FIG. 2. Learning under a constant R

scribed as a curve of 'trial-and-error' learning. The curve for the last 56 problems approaches linearity after trial 2. Curves of similar form have been described as indicators of 'insightful' learning."

67

where m is the number of extinction trials, P_m is the probability of g after the verification of $\bar{x}_m$, P_{m-1} is the probability of g prior to the verification of $\bar{x}_m$, and $\bar{R}$ is the ratio of $P(\bar{x}/\bar{g}h)$ to $P(\bar{x}/gh)$. Figure 3 shows the effect of one negative reinforcement, the verification of $\bar{x}$ (x being found false). The equation for P_m, the probability of g after m successive extinction trials, is

$$P_m = \frac{P_0}{P_0 + \bar{R}_1\bar{R}_2 \cdots \bar{R}_m(1 - P_0)}. \qquad [9]$$

Figure 4 shows the extinction curves for constant values of $\bar{R}$.

It is beyond the scope of this paper to elaborate on all the deductions that may stem from the theory of learning derived from the principle of inverse probability. However, to demonstrate its cogency one example will be given.

What is the relation between the rate of learning and the rate of extinction? We have seen that if R is high the rate of learning is high, and that if $\bar{R}$ is high the rate of extinction is high. The question becomes one of determining the relationship between R and $\bar{R}$.

$$R = \frac{P(x/gh)}{P(x/\bar{g}h)}, \qquad [10]$$

$$\bar{R} = \frac{P(\bar{x}/\bar{g}h)}{P(\bar{x}/gh)}. \qquad [11]$$

Therefore, since $P(x/gh) + P(\bar{x}/gh) = 1$, and
$P(x/\bar{g}h) + P(\bar{x}/\bar{g}h) = 1$,

$$\bar{R} = \frac{1 - P(x/\bar{g}h)}{1 - P(x/gh)}, \qquad [12]$$

thus fixing the relationship between R and $\bar{R}$. To complete the derivation, it is necessary to make an assumption: that as we go from individual to individual, $P(x/gh)$ and $P(x/\bar{g}h)$ are positively correlated. This assumption is nothing more than that persons vary either in their supply of g's, or in their ability to draw x's from the g's that they have. If we make this assumption, then it follows immediately that R and $\bar{R}$ are negatively related, as can be seen from the following table:

Subject	$P(x/gh)$	$P(x/\bar{g}h)$	R	$\bar{R}$
1	.95	.80	1.19	4.00
2	.80	.65	1.23	1.75
3	.65	.50	1.30	1.43
4	.50	.35	1.43	1.30
5	.35	.20	1.75	1.23
6	.20	.05	4.00	1.19

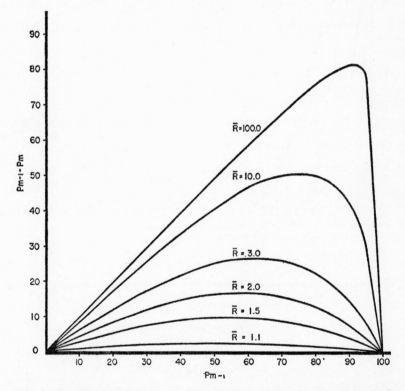

FIG. 3. The amount of decrement, $P_{m-1} - P_m$, as a function of one extinction trial, as a function of P_{m-1} and $\bar{R}$

69

The fact of the negative correlation between rate of learning and rate of extinction has been verified in a number of instances in conditioning studies (Bernstein, 1934; Campbell, 1938; Hunter, 1935; Mateer, 1918).[9] It is also verified by the finding of the Gestalt psychologists that learning which has taken place by insight (R high) is not forgotten as quickly as learning which has

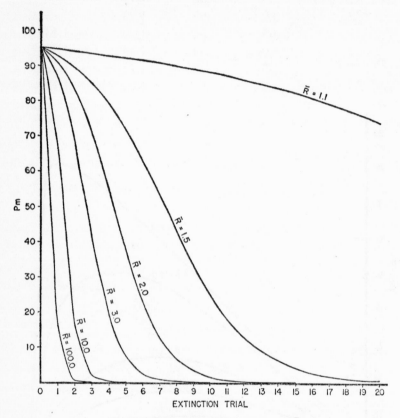

FIG. 4. Extinction under a constant $\bar{R}$

taken place by rote (R low) (Katona, 1940), if we can, at least for the present, equate forgetting with extinction.

Though the primary purpose here is simply to show the

[9] These studies are summarized by Hilgard and Marquis (1940).

possibility of developing a theory of learning on the basis of the principle of inverse probability, taking the principle of inverse probability as a theory of learning has a number of implications with respect to psychological theory.

The method of science as a way of learning. In the opinion of the writer, the most important implication of what has already been said is that by viewing science as a method of learning it is possible to learn something concerning the nature of learning. Whether the principle of inverse probability fully stands up against further scrutiny and empirical data with the interpretations which we have given to g, h, and x is to be seen. The burden of this paper is primarily to show the possibilities inherent in viewing science as a way of learning. Parenthetically it should be pointed out that the very testing of what has been advanced in this paper will employ the principle of inverse probability although it may not employ the particular interpretations of g, h, and x which we have advanced.

The reconciliation of stimulus-response, expectancy, and Gestalt theories. Although, in a sense, this theory of learning we derive from the principle of inverse probability is primarily an expectancy theory, it incorporates some of the most important aspects of stimulus-response theory and Gestalt theory. For one thing, the phenomenon critical for Gestalt theory of learning, the insight phenomenon, is readily yielded as a consequence of the principle of inverse probability. Furthermore, it specifies, in a manner which the Gestalt theorists have not yet specified, the condition under which insight takes place, that is, R is high.

One of the major superiorities of stimulus-response theory over expectancy theory has been the relative docility of the stimulus-response point of view to mathematical quantification, primarily in the hands of Hull and his followers. With the kinds of interpretation of the values which have been developed within the context of probability theory as employed here, the mathematics of probability becomes readily available for the handling of psychological problems. From a mathematical point of view, there is also a distinct superiority in the kind of quantification outlined

71

here. The heart of Hull's theory is in the equation for the learning curve. This was arrived at primarily on the basis of the relatively arbitrary method of curve fitting. There is really no good a priori rationale for determining whether the curve of learning should be a logarithmic or an exponential growth function, as indicated by Hull's own wavering in this matter. On the other hand, the curve of learning which has been advanced in this paper is *necessary* on the basis of the fundamental postulates of probability theory and the interpretation given. One other point of superiority of the learning curve advanced in this paper over that of Hull's exponential growth function is, so to speak, its intuitive propriety. Although the criterion of intuitive propriety is not a necessary one, it is certainly a desirable one. Equation [1] (or better, perhaps, the theorem of compound probability), upon which the remainder is based, formulates what we all, in a sense, "know" to be true. In this respect, Hull's exponential growth function falls considerably short.

Account is taken of effect of "belongingness" on learning. Thorndike (1935) found that it was necessary to take account of the "belongingness" or "relevance" of the reinforcement. When there was belongingness, learning was more rapid than when there was no belongingness. The degree of belongingness is exactly what is expressed by the value of R. If the value of $P(x/gh)$ is large, and $P(x/\bar{g}h)$ is small, then the verification of x "belongs" to g, or is relevant to g, and consequently, as has been indicated, the rate of learning is high.

Consistency with the general nativisim of other theories. According to Thorndike and others, what is learned has, so to speak, to exist at least in small measure in the organism. Thus, in Thorndikean terms, learning consists in the strengthening of already existing connections. If the connections do not exist, at least in small measure, then they cannot be reinforced, and learning cannot take place.

In this respect, the present theory has to assume the very same thing. If learning is the growth of the probability of g, then there must be an initial probability of g which is greater than zero.

72

If the initial probability of *g* is zero, then there can be no increase in the probability of *g* [3].

The possibility of understanding "complex" learning phenomena. Hilgard (1948), in his opening paragraph, suggests that a theory of learning ought to be able to account for such phenomena as "prejudice and bigotry and other learnings which lead to trouble instead of to a satisfactory solution of . . . problems," as well as how skills, preferences, tastes, and knowledge develop. In most learning theories, these "complex" learnings are looked upon as a kind of higher level problem which will be solved after we have solved the problems involved in less "complex" learning. In the theory outlined, it is not necessary to differentiate between lower and higher learnings. The theory applies equally well to the learning of a conditioned response or a prejudice. The issue of molarity versus molecularity vanishes, as does the question of whether reasoning and problem-solving ought or ought not to be considered categories under the general heading of learning. Nor is it necessary to introduce the distinction between primary and secondary reinforcement to explain other than very simple learning.

Hilgard (1948) has formulated six questions about theories of learning which are appropriately asked whenever a "new," or new version of an "old," theory is advanced. The attempt will be made to answer these questions in the light of what has been advanced here.

1. *"What are the limits of learning?"* Although the theory does not provide a contentual answer to this question, it supplies a formal answer. Learning is a function of $P(g/h)$, $P(x/gh)$, and $P(x/\bar{g}h)$. The limits of learning are therefore in terms of the limits of *h*, the generation of *g*'s on the basis of *h*, the generation of *x*'s on the basis of the *g*'s and *h*'s, and whatever is involved in the determination of whether an *x* is or is not to be "tried." (The latter word is borrowed from Hilgard [1948] as he uses it in the concept of "provisional try.") Unless there are *x*'s, and unless the occasion for the verification of *x*'s occurs, learning will not take place.

2. *"What is the role of practice in learning?"* Practice con-

sists in the confirmation and nonconfirmation of x's. Repetition which does not involve the testing of x's will not result in learning. The amount of practice and its quality, the latter defined as the attributes of x, and the associated value of R are determiners of the amount of learning.

3. *"How important are reward, punishment, or other motives in learning?"* They are important in so far as they provide a basis for verifying x's, whose X's involve reward, punishment, or other consequences.

4. *"What is the place of understanding and insight?"* Whether learning is "blind" or "insightful" is a matter of degree as reflected in the magnitude of R.

5. *"Does learning one thing help you learn something else?"* Yes, in so far as the former thing learned has affected the initial probability of g as indicated by formula [4].

6. *"What happens when we remember and when we forget?"* Thus far in our development of the theory, we have only one suggestion to make with respect to this question. It has been shown that on the basis of the theory it follows that there is an inverse relation between R, the rate of learning, and $\bar{R}$, the rate of extinction. Katona's (1940) investigations have shown that if learning is based on principle (R high), there is less forgetting ($\bar{R}$ low). Similar confirmations of the inverse relationship between R and $\bar{R}$ have been found in conditioning studies. Thus, we will remember best what has been learned with R high.

♣ ♣ ♣ ♣ ♣ ♣ **7**

The Exponential
Growth Function
in Herbart and Hull

In the culture of contemporary psychology it is often presumed that the only way in which it is possible to bring mathematical and logical methods to bear in psychology is on the basis of a previous commitment to a behaviorist position. The preceding paper certainly indicates the possibility of a mathematical yet nonbehavioristic approach to some psychological problems. Clark L. Hull's hypothetico-deductive forays have stood as a model of the combination of mathematics and behaviorism; and for some as evidence of the intrinsic necessity in that union. It is thus exceedingly interesting to discover that Hull's fundamental equation for learning, the equation for the change in habit strength as a function of the number of trials, should be essentially the same as the equation used quite a long time ago by Herbart, in his very nonbehavioristic psychology, to express the rise of a concept in consciousness.

Herbart's formula is:[1]

$$\omega = \rho(1 - e^{-rt/\pi})$$

where ω is the amount of the concept in consciousness; π, the total amount of the concept; ρ, the size of the available portion of π; r, the portion of the available assistance from another concept; t, time; and e, the base of natural logarithms.

Hull's (1943) formula is:

$$_sH_R = M(1 - e^{-iN})$$

where $_sH_R$ is habit strength; M, the limit of the growth function, which is itself a function of physiological limit, magnitude of reward, delay of reinforcement, and delay between presentation of the stimulus and the response; e, the base of natural logarithms; i, a constant; and N, number of trials.

[1] *Joh. Fr. Herbart's Sämtliche Werke, 4,* 367–377. This is a combined version of the 1816 and 1834 editions of the *Lehrbuch zur Psychologie.* A more elaborate discussion of the exponential growth function can be found in his *Psychologie als Wissenschaft,* 1824, 5, 368–386).

♣ ♣ ♣ ♣ ♣ ♣ ♣ ♣ *8*

Clinical Psychology
and Logic

There is a prevailing sense of the scientific untenability of clinical psychology among many psychologists. Frequently, clinical psychology is critically envisaged as an art; or if the critic is inclined to be more critical, it may be conceived of as an attempt to obtain knowledge mystically and effect changes magically.

However, a good deal of the difficulty associated with the appropriate scientific delineation and characterization of clinical psychology stems from an inappropriate set of methodological con-

77

siderations, rather than from any essential defect in the various procedures of this branch of our discipline. This should not be interpreted as a statement to the effect that all is well in the house of clinical psychology. Rather, it is intended simply as a suggestion that many of the presumptive ailments, as for example, lack of "experimental" confirmation, are not really what clinical psychology is suffering from.

Let us limit ourselves to one of the major questions associated with clinical psychology: How is it possible for the clinical psychologist to have any notion at all concerning what is going on in the "mind" of the client? There are many circumlocutions whereby this question may be asked to avoid the use of the word "mind." But in the interests of simplicity and in the interests of communication—since the experience of the writer has been that there is less trouble in communication with this word than with many others—we will use the word "mind."

We can, however, formulate our question somewhat more generally and perhaps somewhat more complexly: Is it possible, and in what sense is it possible, for one person to "know" another person's experiences, if experience is, as a certain traditional outlook would have it, utterly and unalterably private? For purposes of discussion we will refer to that position in the field of psychology which denies the possibility of a psychology of experience, on the grounds of the privacy of experience, as behaviorism.

The behaviorist position quickly forces a perplexing antinomy upon our attention, an antinomy of very particular significance to clinical psychology. On the one hand, one of the classical arguments associated with the behaviorist position is a form of the pragmatic argument: That the behaviorist position will lead more quickly and more surely to the satisfaction of the criteria of prediction and control of behavior. On the other hand, there is an atmosphere contemptuous of problems associated with the prediction and control of human behavior that is associated with the behaviorist position. Such problems are regarded as impure, applied, etc., and not quite the proper domain of the "scientist."

This antinomy is not a unique problem of psychologists;

there are other sciences which have been able to bear with grandeur the burden of the analogous antinomy for three hundred years or more.

It is indeed strange, and noteworthy, that among psychologists where the problem is critically that of predicting and controlling human behavior the behavioristic orientation seems to have the least cogency; for when we are interested in predicting and controlling the behavior of a human being the most appropriate questions are: "What is he experiencing?" and "What are his wishes and intentions (conscious or unconscious)?" Somehow this is more satisfying, even from the most pragmatic of points of view, than an enumeration and description of his "habits," or "stimulus-response connections," or "behavior tendencies," etc. It is certainly true that in the history of science our ability to predict and control the behavior of matter has not profited from such questions. But, evidently, our ability to predict and control the behavior of human beings seems to decline as we refrain from attempting to divine the nature of their experiences and motives. The strange thing about this whole situation is that those persons who are most interested in predicting and controlling human behavior, the clinical psychologists, are the very ones who tend to abandon behavioristic modes of thought.

There have been psychologists who have suggested that if you want to predict and control human behavior, perhaps you had better stop trying to be a "scientist," in the orthodox sense. In 1934 Skaggs wrote:

> The writer can see no other conclusion than that scientific psychology is and must be of little *practical value*. At the same time the writer is of the opinion that some of the less scientific psychology is of considerable practical significance. We cannot expect training in scientific experimental psychology to fit one to understand human nature in general. The more scientific the psychologist becomes the more must he retire from the general and complicated problems to more restricted problems and work in isolation from the world at large. There is simply nothing that can be done about the matter. However, the scientific psycholo-

gist might be more tolerant of other students of human nature (practical psychologists, novelists, and the like) because much of their knowledge stands the pragmatic test.

A similar kind of conclusion is arrived at by Rogers in his deeply soul-searching paper, "Persons or Science? A Philosophical Question" (1961).

There are other indications in the literature that the logic of the situation presses on to an "impossible" conclusion; that somehow science, as it is conceived, is perhaps more or less incompatible with prediction and control as far as living organisms are concerned. Hebb (1949), in an article in which he tells how to handle certain kinds of laboratory animals, indicates quite clearly that one is considerably more effective with them if one thinks of their behavior in anthropomorphic terms. And, of course, we must not forget Tolman's classical statement (1938) on how to predict the behavior of rats:

> But, in any case, I, in my future work, intend to go ahead imagining how, *if I were a rat,* I would behave as a result of such and such an appetite and such and such a degree of differentiation; and so on.

Statements such as these, of course, a fortiori indicate a difficulty in the "scientific" approach.

When, as is evident, the press of observations forces us towards a view that there exists a realm of phenomena for which the scientific approach is inappropriate, then we must conclude that the inappropriateness is inherent in what we conceive science to be. In other words, the fact that the present conception of science forces honest, astute, and conscientious investigators to look elsewhere for guidance must be interpreted as a shortcoming in the current conceptions of the scientific approach.

In recent history we have become painfully cognizant of the onslaught on the remainder of our knowledge of the results of cultural, historical, psychological, and sociological investigations and modes of thought. We have gotten into the habit of challenging our presumptive bits of knowledge from a culturological point of view. Perhaps we say to ourselves, "What we believe stems more from our culture, or our need systems, than from what is the case." This kind of doubt has been both devastating and purifying.

We advance the hypothesis that the kind of epistemological scepticism we inherit from the British empiricists, Locke, Berkeley, Hume, and the like, stemmed largely from the state of affairs of their day rather than, say, from the intrinsic necessity of the case. A fundamental characteristic of the thought of the British empiricists is that it conceives of the thinker as essentially alone rather than as a member and participant of a thinking community. Historically, this is indeed both understandable and commendable. These men were pioneers. They were attempting to fashion a world in which they could be free of the traditional prejudices and beliefs. Thus, they were "skeptical" of the knowledge they obtained from their contemporaries; and they found it necessary to dissociate themselves from their less liberated brethren. Furthermore, they were involved in the development of a new system of ethics and metaphysics in which the single individual was supreme, as contrasted with medieval man who was lost in the giant, enveloping embrace of the community. In their hunger for a philosophy of individualism they also generated a philosophy in which community had little or no part, a philosophy to which we might refer as a philosophy of epistemological loneliness.

It was David Hume, the latest of the great figures of British empiricism, who sensed this characteristic most acutely. In the conclusion of Book I of *A Treatise of Human Nature* (1951; pp. 263 ff.), Hume gives expression to the relationship between his isolation and the position he advances. His sense of isolation from the community of men and his reaching out to try to establish communion with the reader are poignant. In the midst of the development of a philosophy in which one of the central distinctions is that between opinion of men and independence of judgment he cries out, ". . . such is my weakness, that I feel all my opinions loosen and fall of themselves, when unsupported by the approbation of others" (264–265).

81

The world in which he lives his life is one which is different from the world he fashions in his philosophy. He writes:

> I dine, I play a game of back-gammon, I converse, and am merry with my friends; and when after three or four hours' amusement, I would return to these speculations, they appear so cold, and strain'd, and ridiculous, that I cannot find in my heart to enter them any farther.

What does this have to do with clinical psychology? Our conceptions concerning the privacy of experience as somehow entailed in the logic of science come from such origins. However, insofar as clinical psychology is concerned, a philosophy of loneliness and estrangement does not seem to be the most appropriate foundation. As a matter of fact, it might not be too great a stretch in characterizing many moderns seeking the assistance of clinical psychologists to say that their disease is exactly this feeling of loneliness and estrangement; that what they are seeking from the relationship with the clinical psychologist is assistance in overcoming the sense of being, as Thomas Wolfe put it, "forever prison pent."

The recognition that intimacy and community between the therapist and client are critical in effecting a cure for the person seeking help must, of course, be put to the credit of Freud's genius and the whole contemporary psychotherapeutic movement. It is worth-while in this connection to listen to what Rogers (1961) has to say about the way in which he conducts psychotherapy. He writes:

> I launch myself into the therapeutic relationship having a hypothesis, or a faith, that my liking, my confidence, and my understanding of the other person's inner world, will lead to a significant process of becoming. I enter the relationship not as a scientist, not as a physician who can accurately diagnose and cure, but as a person, entering into a personal relationship. Insofar as I see him only as an object, the client will tend to become only an object.
> I risk myself, because if, as the relationship deepens, what

develops is a failure, a regression, a repudiation of me and the relationship by the client, then I sense that I will lose myself, or a part of myself. At times this risk is very real, and is very keenly experienced.

I let myself go into the immediacy of the relationship where it is my total organism which takes over and is sensitive to the relationship, not simply my consciousness. I am not consciously responding in a planful or analytic way, but simply in an unreflective way to the other individual, my reaction being based (but not consciously) on my total organismic sensitivity to this other person. I live the relationship on this basis.

Now Rogers is fully aware that this kind of talk is not very "scientific." However, it is unscientific only when we have a science which is based upon the postulate of epistemological loneliness. The behaviorist who understands only the language of behavior might well confront Rogers with the question: "Dr. Rogers, now just what do you mean when you say that you 'risk' yourself? Can you give me an operational definition of risk?" We are certain that Rogers, in all wisdom, should and probably would, refrain from attempting to answer this question. Although he could probably give a genuinely operational definition, he could not give a behavioristic one. In the simple dictionary sense we all know what the meaning of the word "risk" is. Our behaviorist is not simply ignorant. But he may be complexly ignorant in that he consciously refuses to refer Rogers' words to his own "risk" of his personality. As a matter of fact, the avoidance of risk in just this sense in many behavioristically inclined psychologists may be so intense that they cannot deal objectively with the experience of risk.

The behaviorist fashions himself a language which is modeled after the language among strangers. What do we mean? It is characteristic of conversation among strangers that they should talk of the most "public" things. Thus, strangers on a train, say, might talk of the weather, the characteristics of different cities, and the World Series. The language which is used among strangers is generally of the kind which would be accepted by the philosopher of science who calls himself a "physicalist." Thus, the kind of language which is held up to us as an ideal language, that is, a physicalistic language, is one which, in its essence, is not very good for the kind of intimate coparticipation of the kind suggested by Rogers and other clinical psychologists.

On the basis of this discussion let us then say that we are interested in some kind of view of man which, in addition to having some "face validity," will also seem to be more appropriate to the kind of thing clinical psychology is. A tempting position, which we must reject, is that somehow, by some unknown mystical process, we are all involved in some single grand communion. This we reject because it fails to satisfy our common sense, and because it is strongly suggestive of a lack of intellectual discipline of which we cannot help but be suspicious.

However, a simpler and more tenable kind of alternative is the postulate that, after all, we are all pretty much alike. And insofar as we are alike we might be able to "understand" one another by referring each other's expressions to our own experiences; and by some process which, we will say, is very much like the logical process of inference, we predict and thereby control the behavior of the other person.

It may appear that this postulate is either too novel or too vague. Actually it is not at all novel in the field of psychology. It plays a role in every general psychological system. For only if we assume that, after all, we are all pretty much alike, can we have a "general" psychology, a psychology in which the laws, generalizations, abstractions, etc., which are asserted presumably apply to each and every case. And, in the instance of many modern investigations, particularly in the field of learning, the "we" of our postulate is even taken to encompass the white rat. The uniqueness of the individual case is of little concern in a "general" psychology. What matters only are those characteristics in which "after all, we are all pretty much alike." What is novel in our argument is not the postulate itself but that we are carrying it in its implications one step further. So far as its vagueness is concerned, it is sufficiently precise to have functioned admirably in even a less sharply delineated fashion in the history of all "general" psychologies.

Before we enter upon the discussion of logic proper, it is essential that another cultural characteristic of modern science be mentioned and perhaps isolated. Centuries of error and their correction lie behind us. Modern man, for whatever reason, experiences deep humiliation when he finds himself in error. There is a great tendency to avoid this humiliation by refraining from making any assertions except those in which one can place only the highest confidence.

The behaviorist guarantees that he will not make errors in attributing experiences to others by never attributing any experiences to them—at least not in his role as scientist. In the defense of his position he will tell you that he can only know what he has observed. Unfortunately, a critical and basic distinction, that between the "observed" and the "studied," frequently does not bear very much cogency in his thinking. He will assert that since only the behavior of the other person can be observed, only the behavior of the other person can be the object of his study. His parting rejoinder—his last word, so to speak—runs something as follows: "But after all, you can only study the overt behavior of the other one. You cannot study his experiences."

In spite of the compelling quality of such utterances, they are, in the language of the logical positivist, "nonsense." It may be true that one cannot observe anything but the manifest behavior of the other person. But this does not prevent one from studying many other characteristics of the other person. The fact of the matter is that, except in a limited number of latter-day, die-hard, hyperdisciplined studies, most investigators regard the observations of their studies only as a basis for inference about other things. Our knowledge is almost always the result of both observation and inference, and not of observation alone. And if one has to argue that somehow one knows of the other's experiences by observation and other processes, the argument is not unique to the field of psychology.

Our major thesis is that the application of certain forms of formal logic to the thought processes involved in knowing the other

85

person can result in both increasing our understanding of the clinical process as well as supplying the scientific underpinning which many feel that it needs.

In pointing to logic in connection with the clinical processes it is important that it be recognized that we are not thereby also attempting to connect some of the cultural accretions which are generally associated with logic. Thus, for example, the common expression, "cold logic," we feel is quite inappropriate. Hot logic, lukewarm logic, and cold logic can all be quite logical.

Another point of view, with which we are quite out of sympathy, is that which looks toward logic as a substitute for human thought, and which dreams of the day, perhaps, in which it will replace thought. In the way in which we understand logic it is not and cannot be a substitute for the processes of human thinking. There are probably some people in the field of psychology today who envisage the eventual substitution of some kind of logical or mechanical equipment for the clinician. We sincerely hope that these people will gain no comfort from the reading of this discussion.

The application of logic to the processes of thought has had a thorny history, a history which has generated certain prejudices in us about the possibility of using logic in any direct way for understanding the thought processes. When George Boole wrote his famous *The Laws of Thought,* the volume which ushered in the whole train of developments in modern logic, he thought that he was writing what we would call psychology. He thought that the logic as he wrote it was descriptive of the processes of thought which man engaged in. When subsequent investigation dramatically showed that in many instances man's thought was not logical, that man often, so to speak, erred, this particular feature of Boole's contribution became quite discredited. The simple alternative to this is that logic is regarded not as descriptive but as prescriptive. It is to this alternative that most of the work in logic has leaned; and in doing so it has been effectively separated from the discipline of psychology except in some trivial senses.

What we propose here in the way of using logic in the service of psychology is neither exactly descriptive nor exactly prescriptive, although we do not mean to exclude these uses. The alternative we here propose is to use logic, its terms, and its structure, as a heurism whereby we may penetrate more deeply into the nature of the actual processes involved. We consider the logic as somehow representative of the truth of the situation, but we do not assert that it is representative. What we do generally assert, however, is that man engages in processes which are like logical processes; and that by the comparison of the actual processes with the corresponding logical processes, our understanding of these processes may be enhanced. An approach of this kind has been advanced by Piaget (1953).

Let us give an example of the kind of thing which we have in mind. I am standing on the street corner and see a car approaching. I engage in some processes which lead me to the conclusion that I can safely cross if I start right now and that I will be on the other side before the car comes near where I am standing. This whole problem can be completely described in mathematical terms. I can walk so many miles an hour. The distance across the street is such and such of a fraction of a mile. I have the equation that rate times time equals distance. I enter the rate at which I walk, and the distance, and solve the equation for time. Then I estimate the rate at which the car is moving, and the distance it has to go to reach this point, and solve another equation for the time it will take for the car to reach this point. Now, if the time for me to cross turns out to be considerably less than the time for the car to arrive, I conclude that I may cross.

Now actually people generally do not solve problems like this by the solution of equations. They never "think" of equations. But the major point is this: That they engage in psychological processes which are "like" the mathematical processes. There must be some—although not necessarily complete or good—isomorphism between the processes in which they have engaged and the mathematical ones.

If we should be interested in gaining an understanding of the nature of this kind of judgment, of what factors make a difference in it, etc., the knowledge of the equations, of the mathematics of the situation, would be basic equipment. For by the comparison of the mathematics with the actual thought processes we can come to understand the thought processes. This would be a use of mathematics in a way in which we assert neither that it is descriptive of, nor prescriptive for, the actual processes.

We have talked of logic generally. However, there is a technical problem of choice among different logics. This is not the place to enter into a discussion of the variety of and relations among the various logics available. The choice for the purposes for which we intend it must be based upon some apprehension of the fittingness of the important characteristics of the logical system to the important characteristics of the situation to which it is being applied— and upon some sense of the cogency of outcome of such an application. The marriage of a logic with some other enterprise may be either barren or productive of weaklings if the mating is improper.

In our earlier discussion we suggested that knowledge of the other one is somehow to take place by reference to one's own experience. Now, for our present purposes, experiences on the part of the clinical psychologist which are unconscious must be considered as nonexistent. Thus, before we can talk about either logic or the clinical situation in any detail, we must presuppose that we have a clinical psychologist to whom a large variety of his experiences are available in consciousness. From a psychoanalytic point of view we might speak of an individual in whom many of the repressions have been overcome so that he is able to hold in consciousness, without immediately repressing them, ideas usually revulsive such as, for example, incest wishes, etc. Thus, for this kind of clinician, the task involved in understanding the other person essentially involves the attribution of one or another of his experiences with a probability value indicative of the likelihood that this is the experience in the client to which the client is referring. It should be evident that whereas our view in general calls for a clinician in whom the appropriate experiences are conscious, it does not necessarily call for the same in the client.

It would seem that the most appropriate logic would be one which is probabilistic in nature. However, it is indeed a very special kind of probability. It cannot be probability in a relative frequency sense since, without stretching a point, there are no samples or populations sufficiently homogeneous from which a sensible ratio may be made; nor does the clinical approach, which is so very much concerned with the particular event, or particular experience under consideration, seem a particularly fitting roost for a frequency-theory probability. The probability notion with which we might have some business has more to do with degree of certainty than with objective states of affairs.

It is rather unfortunate for our purposes that probability is too often conceived of as a branch of mathematics rather than of logic. The view that probability is primarily a form of logic rather than of mathematics goes back to Leibniz and finds its current expression in the work of John Maynard Keynes (1948).

The logical problem involved in clinical psychology is the making of inferences about experiences from overt behavior. The inference may be made, for example, that the individual is experiencing pain from observing him saying "ouch!" Now this may or may not be a valid inference in any given situation. It is indeed possible that a person will say "ouch" even if he is not in pain, as, for example, in the case of malingering. Let us examine the conditions of such an inference. The degree to which we will accept the notion that the person who says "ouch" is in pain is contingent upon a series of other judgments we make, and therefore we call this a problem in inference.

Let us now introduce the word "probability," to indicate the degree of tenability to be associated with a proposition. Immediately it becomes evident that the probability that the man is in pain depends upon the probability that he would say "ouch" if he were in pain, and inversely dependent on the probability that he would say "ouch" whether or not he were in pain. It is also evident that the tenability of the proposition that the man is experiencing pain is based on other considerations than whether he does or does not say "ouch." If, for example, we could see his wound we would maintain that it was highly probable that he was experiencing pain.

The essence of our judgment concerning the experience of the other person on the basis of his overt behavior is our estimate of the contingency of the overt behavior on experience. The logic of the relations among these judgments seems to be most adequately handled by the principle which is the basic one for nonfrequency theories of probability, the so-called principle of inverse probability, or the Rule of Bayes; and, the greatest portion of our understanding of the contingency of overt behavior on experience comes from self-observation. It is in a combination of inference through the use of inverse probability and self-observation that knowledge concerning the experience of the other person is possible.

The principle of inverse probability has been discussed, and the possibility of the use of the principle as a general theory of learning has been outlined.[1] The notion was advanced that one of the critical features involved in learning was a ratio, which was called R. R has many properties in common with what is called a likelihood ratio in contemporary statistical theory.

For our purposes we will rewrite R as follows:

$$R = \frac{P(B_o/E_oh)}{P(B_o/\bar{E}_oh)}$$

to be read as "The probability of behavior B_o on experience E_o, over the probability of B_o on not-E_o, all under conditions h." These probabilities can be ascertained by the individual only on the basis of some kind of self-observation, for behavior and experience together are available only to a person himself.

According to the logic of inverse probability, the probability of E_o on B_o varies directly with R. In other words, the probability of the experience E_o on the basis of observing behavior B_o depends directly on $P(B_o/E_o)$ and inversely on $P(B_o/\bar{E}_o)$. If this

[1] See pp. 58 ff.

ratio is large, then the clinician is more inclined to attribute the experience E_o to the individual.

The critical reader will have observed that we have passed easily from E_o and B_o as characteristic of the clinician to having them both characteristic of the client. This technical weakness disappears if it is indeed true that "after all, we are all pretty much alike"; and this technical weakness would make everything we have said complete nonsense if it is false. However, willy-nilly the clinician must be doing something like this. In the last analysis, only the clinician's sense that we are all alike in the more important respects can make tenable either the theory which is being advanced or the kind of therapy talked of by persons like Rogers, the psychoanalysts, etc.

In a paradoxical way the theory not only accounts for correct judgments on the part of the clinical psychologist but also for incorrect ones. It shows how, for example, a clinical psychologist may be "riding a hobby," that is, explaining wide ranges of behavior on the basis of a limited range of experiences. In a given clinician, the probability of behavior on the basis of a given experience may run very high compared to the probability of that behavior on the basis of other experiences. That is, for a given behavior and a given experience, the R-value is high. This clinician will be inclined to attribute this kind of experience with great certainty, because in himself this R-value is high. It is here that the education of the clinical psychologist is extremely important. What his education should do is to show him the plausibility, within himself, of alternative behaviors on the basis of given experiences, and the multiplicity of experiences which may give rise to some specific kind of behavior. If, as has been suggested before, the task of the clinical psychologist is that of finding to which experiences within himself he is to refer the given item of behavior which he observes, it is extremely important that his training shall open up to consciousness the wide ranges of experiences that lie within him. This, of course, is one way of conceiving of the desirability of having psychotherapy for one who is to do psychotherapy.

One of the major problems which faces the clinical psychologist in his daily work is that of relevance. He hears a case history, or listens to his client tell him of many things. Somehow some things which he hears "matter" more than others. As the flow is taking place a vast variety of experiences within the clinician come to be referred to in this complex relationship. Some of the clinician's experiences are brought into focus. Others of them seem to fall out of focus. Then there is the vast amount of experiential material within the clinician which has somehow been untouched by the contact with the client.

What we have said in the above paragraph may be clarified by bringing to bear upon it one of the lessons of probability theory of Keynes. Keynes has an eminently simple definition of relevance which catches the essence of the process to which we are referring. Recasting it into the symbols we have used, an item of behavior B_o is relevant to an experience E_o if the probability of E_o is modified with the introduction of B_o.

In and of itself this may not appear to be very cogent. However, the use of this formulation can help us in seeing just exactly what the effect of clinical experience may be, and is suggestive of a kind of case-history type of research which may be extremely valuable in opening up previously unseen relevancies. One of the best examples of this kind of research is presented to us in a paper by Josephine Hilgard (1953).

She points out that in the study of several cases of rather sudden precipitation of psychoses, the ages of the children of the patients were not considered to be particularly relevant. Then it became apparent that these patients' children were at an age at which the patients themselves had had rather severe traumatic experiences.

This readily becomes: The probability of becoming psychotic increases as a result of beholding intimately my child who is now as old as I was when (say) my parents died; and by our definition of relevance the age of the child has become relevant. It should be apparent from this that when we say that we are all pretty much alike it does not mean that we must all be psychotic, nor that we must all have children, nor that we must all have had the experience of our parents dying. Nor in point of fact need we have had these experiences. But rather in the way in which all yearning is the same, and all pain is the same, and all fantasy is the same, etc.—only in this way need we have had these experiences. And the method whereby we may become aware of the relationship between experience and behavior is through the use of systematic self-observation.

♣ ♣ ♣ ♣ ♣ ♣ ♣ ♣ ♣ *9*

A Reconsideration
of the Problem
of Introspection

The question of the scientific propriety of the method of introspection should be rethought in the perspective of modern times.
Two related considerations are involved. The first is a sense of
society's need for a psychology more appropriate to its problems.
The second is a conviction that, although psychologists should be
methodologically careful, they should not afford themselves the lux-
ury of methodological snobbery. There is no investigatory method
which is "pure" and which provides an absolute guarantee against

94

the commission of error. It may indeed be, as one of my students once aptly put it, that the correlation between purity and fertility must at least be negative. If errors be committed, we look to the future for their correctives. In the meantime, and perhaps ultimately, we accept a pragmatic criterion.

It is characteristic in the history of ideas that when some notion is rejected, even for adequate cause, many seemingly associated notions get rejected with it. Often these associated notions may be sound. Such has been the case with introspection. In the outright rejection of the method of introspection, much that was of considerable value was rejected.

In spite of the avowed rejection of the method, it has stayed with us, in several disguised forms. As Boring (1953) has indicated, "introspection is still with us, doing its business under various aliases, of which *verbal report* is one." Boring seems relatively uncritical of the manner in which we contemporarily avail ourselves of introspection. The argument here is for a careful and avowed use of introspection.

In less disguised form introspection is with us in contemporary clinical psychology. The method of introspection is the method that the patient uses, although there is little avowed recognition of it as the method of the clinician, except perhaps among the psychoanalysts (for example, Reik, 1948). However, "therapy" is coming to be viewed as appropriate training for the aspirant clinician even in nonpsychoanalytic contexts.

The rejection of the method of introspection is coincident with the inception of behaviorism in America. The first important behavioristic pronunciamento took place in 1913 (Watson, 1913). It is important to understand the immediate antecedents of behaviorism in order to understand the wide popularity it gained. Boring's comprehensive history makes it unnecessary to recount the involved circumstances associated with the death of classical introspection. Boring (1953) believes that it "went out of style . . . because it had demonstrated no functional use and therefore seemed dull, and also because it was unreliable."

Psychology was in the throes of the Würzburg-Cornell

struggle in the first decade of the twentieth century. The Würz-burgers had discovered imageless thoughts; and they themselves hardly knew what to do with them. Titchener, at Cornell, sensed the staggering implications of the Würzburg findings, and strug-gled desperately to reject them (1909).

The psychological literature of the time is in many respects confused, repetitive, and—we might say—anguished. Psychology had, it seemed, got itself into absolutely inextricable difficulties; and there was no one within the introspective movement who had the clarity of vision to go beyond these difficulties. Watson, for all the limitations that we may ascribe to him, had clarity and offered a program psychologists could follow.

Let us briefly examine the nature of some of the Würzburg findings. They discovered that thought was possible without images; and that thought was guided by states variously designated by the terms *Aufgabe, Bewusstseinslage,* and *determinierende Tendenz.* The favored method was the *Ausfragemethode.* Mayer and Orth (1901) use the method of free association to a verbal stimulus, instructing the subject to report *everything* that went on between the hearing of the stimulus word and the making of the response. Messer (1906) finds himself forced to posit *unconscious* processes underlying the processes of thought. Ach (1905) introduces the concept of the will, that is, motivation, as guiding the thought processes; he uses a probing investigatory procedure; and he uses hypnosis. Bühler (1907) indicates that it is important, in the study of the thought processes, to empathize and sympathize with the sub-jects engaged in this kind of experimentation.

Then the problem is dropped like the proverbial hot po-tato. Külpe, the leading figure in the Würzburg movement, leaves Würzburg and goes to Bonn in 1909, and the work practically ceases. Bühler posthumously publishes Külpe's lectures which, ac-cording to Boring (1950), "contain a pretty complete system of psychology. But the chapter on thought was missing! Bühler said that Külpe had not been lecturing on the topic."

In the light of the foregoing, and in the light of what we have learned from psychoanalysis, a rather simple explanation suggests itself. These investigators were using themselves and each other as subjects. They had struck the unconscious, and particularly unconscious motivation, and had to probe it if they were to make any headway. However, as we know today, probing the unconscious tends to generate anxiety and resistance; and these investigators simply were not prepared to undergo the necessary personal trials involved. Boring (1953) suggests a relationship between the Würzburg school and Freud, but makes little of it.

Psychology had two possible alternatives: either to widen its investigations to take account of and to study the role of unconscious motivation on the thought processes, or to detour. Academic psychology detoured; and detoured in two ways: It detoured by way of behaviorism, completely rejecting (at least avowedly) the whole method of introspection, and it detoured by way of Gestalt psychology. The former dropped the whole concept of mind, conscious and unconscious. The latter adopted as a basic principle that whatever introspection is done should be naive introspection, with no probing and no analysis, thus preventing intrusion upon the unconscious.

Perhaps one of the most important distinctions necessary for the understanding of the nature of introspection is the classical one between the experience and what is experienced. It is the distinction contained in the classical one of *Kundgabe* versus *Beschreibung* (Boring, 1953). It is the distinction the psychoanalyst makes when he concerns himself primarily with a memory, as contrasted with the event to which the memory presumably refers.

The distinction is somewhat difficult to grasp when we deal with perception. Let us consider a simple experience reported as "I see a book." From the point of view of this distinction it is one or another of two reports: "I *see* a book," or "I see a *book*." In the first instance it is a report of experience as experience. In the second instance the reference is to the object rather than to the experience of the object. One may be true, and the other false, as, for example, in a hallucination.

The distinction is easier to make when we consider something like anxiety. It is hard to make when the experience involves

97

an external stimulus. It is of interest that when Washburn (1922) made her presidential address before the American Psychological Association in 1921 she felt that it was necessary to say that introspection is proper only where there is an external stimulus. This, she believed, would endow introspection with "objectivity"—an unfortunate semantic identification of "object" with "objectivity." It is here, probably, when the Watsonian noose was drawing very tight around the neck of introspection, that introspection surrendered the very thing which was its major merit. Introspection has its maximum value on those very experiences for which there may be no conspicuous physical stimuli, such as grief, joy, anxiety, depression, exhilaration, anger, etc.

A major criticism which has been leveled against the method of introspection is that the data of introspection are not public. In the case of overt behavior it is possible, at least in principle, for two observers to observe a given phenomenon simultaneously. This has sometimes been referred to as the criterion of publicity; and it has been said that data are not acceptable unless this criterion has been satisfied (again, at least in principle).

That introspective data are not public in this sense is not to be questioned. What is to be questioned is whether the criterion is essential. What is the value of the criterion of publicity? Its value, presumably, inheres in the conviction that it avoids error and provides for verification. However, can we not have verification without publicity? Let us consider one of the most acceptable kinds of investigatory procedure from this point of view, the conditioning experiment. There is no way of verifying Pavlov's experiments today by having another observer watching them, since, to say the least, Pavlov's dogs are quite dead. To verify Pavlov's findings we would have to get other dogs. Furthermore, the fact that two people could have stood by to count the number of drops of saliva is quite irrelevant. If the criterion of publicity is not met by introspection, it is not really very serious as long as each scientist has, so to speak, at least one "dog" he can observe directly.

The crisis generated by disparate results from Würzburg and Cornell, with the one finding imageless thoughts and the other not finding them, was hardly adequate reason for the total rejection of introspection. Disparate results from different laboratories are usually provocative of further investigation, rather than the occasion for dropping the problems, the methods, and the fundamental points of view involved. The failure of the introspective method to satisfy this naive criterion of publicity could hardly have been the real reason for the rejection of introspection as a method.

A more important problem is the possibility of publicity, not of the data, but of the report. Even though the process of introspective observation is, in a sense, private, the information gleaned from the observations must be public. This raises the question of language and communication. There are two questions that may be asked in connection with language with respect to introspection: First, if we relate our introspections to one another, would we understand one another? Second, if we do understand one another, how does this come to pass? If the answer to the first question is to any degree affirmative, then to that extent is the criterion of publicity of report satisfied.

For the answer to the first question we appeal, at the very least, to common sense. If we hear a person say, "I am sorry," or "I am worried," or "I feel sick," etc., there is hardly any question but that we understand what he means. There are times when we may not believe him; but the possibility of fraud, intentional or unintentional, or lack of precision exists with respect to any methodology. The fact is, however, that we understand him.

The answer to the second question now becomes a matter for empirical investigation. This is not the place to enter into a detailed discussion of the psychology of language learning. However, it is extremely pertinent to indicate that the theory of language learning implicit in contemporary behavioristics is much more simple than is consistent with the facts. This implicit theory may be roughly characterized as follows:

The teacher holds up a ball and says, "Ball." The learner repeats, "Ball." The learner then, presumably, comes to "know" the meaning of the word. Certainly the theory is stretched to the breaking point when confronted with the fact that we all fairly well understand the meaning of words such as "sorrow," "feeling," "nausea," "if," "but," etc.

Titchener (1921) wrote an essay which, in part, attempted to present to English-speaking readers some of the contributions of Franz Brentano. In the judgment of the writer, Brentano is one of the most important figures in the history of psychology. The major work of Brentano with respect to psychology (1874) has not, as far as could be determined by the writer, been translated into English. Of Brentano and Wundt, Titchener wrote: "The student of psychology, though his personal indebtedness be also twofold, must still make his choice for one or the other. There is no middle way between Brentano and Wundt." For the most part, the choice of the classical introspectionists was for Wundt. Wundt and Brentano published their major psychological works at about the same time. Two major schools of thought issue from Brentano. One is the already mentioned Würzburg school. The other is psychoanalysis, with Brentano having been the only academic psychologist under whom Freud studied (Merlan, 1945; 1949). Psychoanalysis, however, differed from the Würzburgers with respect to a readiness to face the unconscious. It may have been easier for Freud to break through to the unconscious because of some of the special circumstances of Freud's life and career (see Bakan, 1958).

Brentano, Külpe, and Freud conceived of introspection not so much as of the present, but of the past. They took seriously what was then a common observation, that introspection at the moment an experience is taking place changes the character of that experience. If we are interested, say, in anger, then introspection at the moment of anger tends to reduce the anger. It is only when anger is past that it can be properly examined. Using the method of introspection, thus avowedly retrospectively, makes it possible to examine psychological phenomena which cannot readily be elicited in the laboratory, except perhaps with very great ingenuity.

This difficulty of the introspection of Wundt and Titchener was adequately recognized by McDougall (1922), who wrote: "Experimental introspection has obvious limitations. Many of our most vital and interesting experiences, such as grief or joy or fear or moral struggle, cannot be induced at will, except perhaps in very slight degrees. And, under the most favorable conditions, introspection of our more vivid and vital experiences is difficult, because we are apt to be primarily interested in the events of the outer world in which we are taking part, if only as observers. Then again the very act of introspection does to some extent modify the experiences we wish to observe and describe; so that in introspecting we partially defeat our own purposes."

Thus, the type of introspection which was advocated by Titchener, and which was the object of attack by the anti-introspectionists, was a type which, by its nature, could not attack the important aspects and kinds of experience. The cry that a psychology was wanted which would have some usefulness was completely justified when the object of attack was the kind of introspection advocated by Titchener.

A characteristic of good science is that it is ever alert to the possibility of the commission of systematic types of errors. One of the major criticisms leveled against introspection is that its results are untrustworthy.

There is a respect in which introspective observations are more trustworthy than observations made by the use of the sense organs. Sense organs may be defective. Sense organs are subject to illusion. Observations made with the sense organs are subject to the accidents of angle of regard, kind of illumination, noise level, etc. In the last analysis, the sense organs are subject to hallucination. Introspection is a method which does not involve the sense organs in the usual fashion, and therefore all of the error tendencies associated with the sense organs simply do not exist for introspection.

However, introspection has associated with it other sources of error. But even at this date, we have achieved a certain amount of progress in isolating them. We know about the stimulus-error. We are aware of the tendency to suppress data (repression), of the tendency to supply socially acceptable data in place of other data (distortion, rationalization, displacement, etc.). But, insofar as we are aware of these error tendencies, we can take precautions against

101

their commission. In this respect introspection is no different from any other set of methods in science. To be aware, for example, of the tendency toward rationalization stimulates us to challenge our introspective findings to determine whether they have resulted from the rationalization process. It is a matter of time and careful work to discover other error sources. We have discovered suggestion, cultural determination, ethnocentrism, etc.; and the list will probably lengthen as our experience with the method enlarges.

Psychoanalysis has one major limitation with respect to our purpose which was not present in classical introspection. This is that the major objective of psychoanalysis is therapy.[1] The major objective of the classical introspectionists was the acquisition of knowledge. This is a fundamental difference.

Essentially, what is being advocated in this paper is the use of the psychoanalytic method with the objective of the classical introspectionists.

It has been indicated that what is being advocated in this paper is partly on the grounds of the need for a science of psychology with practical implication. However, there is an old lesson in the history of science of which we avail ourselves. Whereas knowledge may have practicality as its ultimate objective, it has been found that we sometimes do better, both practically and theoretically, if we temporarily forsake the practical objective.

In taking the objective from the classical introspectionists, it is necessary to make some modification in the psychoanalytic procedure. Although the investigator should be "free" in his associations, he should not permit himself to wander too far from the subject under investigation. His associations should stay under the influence of the task at hand. Of course, as in any investigation, decisions of relevance have to be made, and sometimes only a dim intuition dictates the nature of these decisions. Although there is no a priori method for determining relevance, the investigator

---

[1] This is true even though Freud (1929) did envisage that "the future will probably attribute far greater importance to psychoanalysis as the science of the unconscious than as a therapeutic procedure."

should always attempt to keep in mind that he is serving science primarily and himself secondarily.

In accordance with what has already been said the writer attempted to conduct an investigation of the kind suggested. It is a "miniature" investigation in that it was conducted only over a very short period of time, five days for about an hour and a half each day.

There were several reasons for the choice of the topic: retention and revelation of secrets. One of these is that the topic seemed more amenable to introspection than to other methods. By its very nature a secret is something that may not reflect itself in overt behavior. Another reason for the choice of the topic is that it seems fundamental for any kind of introspective investigation. It seemed important to obtain information concerning the nature of secret retention and secret revelation before very much progress could be made with other topics. A third reason was that the topic seemed to lie close to the oft-stated objective of psychology as being prediction and control of human behavior.

The procedure simply involved sitting down to the typewriter and typing whatever came, after the decision concerning the topic was made. The choice of the typewriter was made primarily on the basis that the writer has found himself to be more fluent this way than either writing by hand or talking into a recording machine.

By virtue of the nature of the subject chosen, the writer attempted to write "as though" the material would never be released. Under any circumstances, even if this was a myth, the sense of the possibility of editing was not mythical. At the moment the writer does not consider it wise to release the protocol. However, one example will be given. The following is taken from the record with some editing:

. . . What is one of the secrets such as *thee and me* have? I once talked to a professor of zoology at lunch about the academic life. He commented that over the head of every academician hangs a sword on a thin string. No matter how much you do, you never feel that you are doing enough. I am reminded of Freud's dream of Irma's injection. He says, "I am always careful, of course, to see that the syringe is perfectly clean. *For I am conscientious.*" The italics are mine. If he felt that he were really conscientious, if he had no feelings of shortcomings in this connection, why did he have to protest that he *was* conscientious? The guilt of lack of conscientiousness haunts most of my friends. My lack of conscientiousness is my "secret." But here I find myself confessing to lack of conscientiousness. But I was not able to do so until I was able to remember something which would make it possible for me not to have my guilt alone. I brought up the zoology professor. When I wrote the above line about him I hesitated for a moment on the question of whether or not to use quotation marks, or to write it in the way that I did. The quotation marks would have had to come, in all honesty, after the word "string." I wrote on, however, "No matter how much you do, you never feel that you are doing enough." This is what I would have liked him to have said. I added it to give the impression that he had said it, but not quite lying about it.

I think that what has been said above can be generalized. *We are more prone to confess a secret guilt when we can believe that others have the same secret guilt. . . .*

The general pattern involved in this kind of writing is that of an oscillation between a free expressive mood and an analytic mood, with the free expression being the subject of the analysis. The question of what a given item of free expression might mean with respect to the major topic under investigation was repeatedly asked.

In the course of this investigation a series of propositions, including the italicized one above, were formulated. This list can be considered to be the yield of this "miniature" investigation:

1. (Given above.)

2. Persons with a secret guilt tend to create situations in which they can "see" that others have the same secret guilt.

3. A secret is a secret by virtue of the anticipation of negative reactions from other people.

4. A secret is maintained in order to maintain some given perception of one's self in others.

5. Persons who associate with one another in the context of a larger group, who have a secret from that larger group, will create a metaphorical or otherwise cryptographic language in which to discuss the secret.

6. To conceal a secret, one may tend to reveal a fabricated "secret," or a less-secret secret, in order to generate the impression that one is being open and frank.

7. One of the important secret areas in our culture is in connection with our intellectual limitations.

8. When an individual has a secret he will attempt to "protest" that the opposite is the case, if the secret has an opposite.

9. The revelation of a secret may involve the attempt to generate the impression that one is telling a joke, to achieve the double purpose of revelation on the one hand and disbelief on the other.

10. In the revelation of a secret, one may attempt to generate the impression that one degrades one's self in one's own eyes, in order to reduce the degradation that one anticipates will be the reaction of others to the revelation.

11. If A knows a secret about B, and B knows a secret about A, and if A discovers that B has revealed A's secret, then A will be inclined to reveal B's secret.

12. If an individual changes his group identification from Group A to Group B, and if Group A has a secret which it keeps from Group B, that individual will be inclined to reveal Group A's secret to the members of Group B.

The simple fecundity of the method soon became evident. After the decision was made to attempt it and a brief beginning was made, it became apparent that this was, to use a term from the vernacular, a veritable mine of information. Essentially it capitalizes on the fact that the investigator has had twenty or thirty or forty or fifty or sixty or seventy years for the collection of various kinds of information. Certainly one of the defects of this kind of data collection is that it is not systematic in the usual way in which we understand this term. Yet it is the result of years of trial and error, of a kind which most laboratory types of investigation do not generally get. It may be argued that these data have been uncritically gathered. This is a valid point. However, the necessary criticality can be supplied in the course of the investigation itself.

This kind of investigation can be severely hampered by what may be loosely designated as "ethical" considerations. Let us consider, for example, the proposition that a secret is maintained in order to maintain a given perception of one's self in others. By virtue of the intimate connection between ethics, in this larger sense, and the kind of data which may become the subject of an introspective investigation, it is extremely important that the investigator attempt, to the degree that he can, to divest the investigation of ethical considerations. Methodologically this divesture may involve a preliminary investigation of the ethical considerations themselves. Also, it must be added that, for some kinds of problems to be investigated by these methods, less may be required in the way of preliminary investigation than for other problems. However, for the investigation of any problem by these methods, a scientific and objective attitude is a prerequisite.

One of the major merits of this kind of approach is that it studies the phenomena of psychology directly, in a manner rarely the case in most psychological investigations. Actually, the kind of material which issues from an introspective investigation such as is being advocated is presupposed in many other psychological investigations. Consider for the moment the "lie" scale of the Minnesota Multiphasic Personality Inventory. The test presumably "gets at" the kind of thing which has been investigated in the investigation on secrets cited above. However, the items of this scale were selected because they would presumably be answered negatively by persons who were trying to put themselves "in the most acceptable light socially" (Hathaway and McKinley, 1951). This presumes, with little qualification, the content of the fourth proposition above, as well as about fifteen preconceptions concerning the meaning of social acceptability. (There are 15 items in the "lie" scale.)

Furthermore, had the makers of the MMPI critically examined the nature of secrets in the way in which it has been begun in the above investigation, they would have seen that there are other dynamics of lying, in addition to the one of which they did avail themselves. For example, proposition 6 indicates that a certain amount of truth-telling may simply be a device for "covering up" one or more other lies. It may well be that the operation of the dynamic indicated by proposition 6 acts to depress the "lie" score when lying is really taking place. A full awareness of the kind of thing that issues from such an investigation can greatly enhance the effectiveness even of pencil-and-paper tests.

From a more theoretical point of view, if we seriously accept the mission of psychology as being that of the prediction and control of human behavior, the psychology of secrets is an important link in the chain of psychological findings and theory. Investigators, no matter what they are investigating, must be cognizant, at the very least, of the possibility of dissemblance when they use human subjects. To predict and control an individual's behavior it is important to know, for example, his group identifications, his objectives, his values, etc. Many of these items of information are secret. They may even be secret to the subject himself. And under any circumstances they are not items which will be revealed readily. Thus, until psychologists develop a rather full understanding of the dynamics of this phenomenon, ignorance of it will stand in the way of other investigations.

The above paragraph would be considerably less cogent if the phenomenon of the secret played only a small role in connection with other phenomena. However, secrets play their most important role in those phenomena which are most vital. A psychology that seeks to understand these vital phenomena must have an appreciation of the phenomena of secret retention and secret revelation. Whether we are interested in the problems of marriage, international affairs, politics, military strategy, litigation, business practices, economics, etc., the psychology of secrets is extremely pertinent. And the psychology of secrets yields most effectively to the method which is being proposed.

Although the psychology of secrets is perhaps a central and basic one associated with the method, investigations could and should be pursued with great profit on other problems. Thus, for example, problem solving and decision making can and should be investigated by the method of retrospective analysis. Investigations on status, power, anxiety, fear, aggression, aesthetic experience, learning, communication, memory, concept formation, perception, judgment, charity, loneliness, betrayal, etc., could and should be carried out to enhance our understanding of these phenomena.

Perhaps the critical question in the mind of the reader up to this point is that of the validity of the findings of an introspective investigation. The problem of validity has already been discussed, but somewhat abstractly.

The propositions which issued from the "miniature" investigation are what may be considered to be hypotheses for investigation by other methods. Thus, at the very least, the method may be recommended as a device for systematically getting hypotheses as contrasted with, say, the casual reaching out for a pair of variables and hypothesizing a relationship between them.

Again, as has already been indicated, it may be used as a method whereby an investigator can bring his presuppositions concerning an investigation to formulation; where he can critically examine his presuppositions; and where he might be helped in conceiving of other presuppositions against which he can contrast the ones he is using. Or the method could be used as a device whereby an investigator, having gotten some experimental results which he cannot understand, provokes his imagination to arrive at some kind of explanation of his results. The deliberate and avowed adoption of the method would be extremely helpful in these respects.

However, the writer believes that the method warrants more than this. As has been indicated, the method has a directness not to be found in any other method of investigation of psychological phenomena. In any investigation each thing lying between the phenomenon and the data is a source of error. These sources of error are minimized by the method being proposed. All errors such as failure of the subject to cooperate (for example, rehearsal when instructed not to do so in studies on reminiscence), dissemblance, failure to comprehend instructions, refusal to believe the expressions of the investigator's avowed intentions, fear of hidden—or manifest—microphones, lack of skill on the part of the subject (like fixating on a point in a vision experiment), refusal to take a "naive" attitude (in Gestalt experiments), the lack of control over human subjects (such as subjects in problem-solving studies already knowing the solutions to problems but not informing the investigator), subjects knowing the intention of the investigator (such as subjects knowing that the experimenter is interested in demonstrating a relation between frustration and aggression, and therefore concealing their felt aggression), etc., are minimized in this kind of investigation.

The propositions which were yielded by the "miniature" investigation also have a certain kind of self-evidence associated with them. They elicit the "of course" response. Some of the propositions may require further specification and further qualification. Nevertheless, they are in some sense obvious. It is the sense of self-evidence which is associated, perhaps, with the axioms of Euclidean geometry. The nature of self-evidence is, of course, an extremely difficult problem and perhaps more properly falls in the province of the philosopher. Or, perhaps, self-evidence is a problem to be investigated by the very methods here proposed. However, whatever the ultimate nature of self-evidence may be, there is a sense in which the results of an introspective investigation are of this type.

Now, of course, the matter of self-evidence may be challenged by the question: Self-evident to whom? In one respect this is a valid question. But in another respect it is not. It is valid in that if we are to know that it is self-evident it must be self-evident to someone. However, when the mathematician uses the term "self-evident" he means something which is intrinsic to the proposition, rather than something dependent upon the reader or the hearer of the proposition. For the mathematician it is the self-evidence of the proposition which makes it possible for the person to see the self-evidence, rather than the reverse. It is this characteristic which is shared by introspective propositions.

As a matter of fact, some of the propositions which issued from the "miniature" investigation seem to partake of greater self-evidence than others. Thus, for example, proposition 4 seems to be quite self-evident, whereas proposition 5 seems to be somewhat less self-evident. And even the seeming self-evidence of proposition 4 may be quite culture-bound. However, what has been reported is only an extremely limited investigation, only a beginning and only a sample. Nevertheless, what has been presented is enough to suggest the possibility of achieving the kind of self-evidence that has been indicated.

Two related, but distinguishable, problems are those of replication and generality. Can such an investigation be replicated? The answer is affirmative, although the difficulties of replication should be recognized and account should be taken of them. If an investigator attempts to replicate his own investigation at another time, he will inevitably be under the influence of what he has already done. In replicating such an investigation, the very replication itself should come under the scrutiny of the investigator. He should challenge, for example, his personal identification with the results he has already obtained, and prepare himself for finding both novelty and contradiction with respect to his earlier investigation. If one investigator is interested in replicating the investigation of another investigator, he should carefully take into account the possibility of suggestion, or of his willingness to accept the results of the earlier investigator (particularly if the first investigator has prestige for the second investigator). He should take careful cognizance of possible motivation for showing the earlier investigator to be in error, etc. In some instances it may be extremely worth while to investigate some topic without reading the results of the earlier investigation until the completion of the second investigation, making a comparison later on. Carefully controlled experimentation to determine possible effects of suggestion, for example, is extremely feasible.

110

The generality of the results of such an investigation is somewhat more difficult, but the difficulty is not unique to introspective investigation. One investigator's results can be compared with another investigator's results, so that the problem of uniqueness with respect to a single investigator is vitiated. However, one may ask, in the event of consistency of results among a group of investigators, may the findings not be unique to a group of persons all of whom are introspective investigators? There is no easy answer to this problem. However, we face the same problem in other investigations. May not the results of studies in rote learning be largely unique to college sophomores? May not the results of studies in, say, secondary reinforcement be unique to rats, or more particularly laboratory rats, or even more particularly white laboratory rats, or still more particularly tamed white laboratory rats, etc.? May not all findings concerning mental abnormality be unique to mentally abnormal persons contacted by investigators, and may not these very contacts be a major determinant of the findings?

The answer, of course, to each of these questions is contingent upon some decision concerning relevance, a decision that has to be made in connection with any investigation. Actually, the kind of investigation being advocated has an advantage in this respect over other kinds of investigation. For, in an introspective investigation the very decisions concerning relevance can come under the same scrutiny as the phenomena being investigated.

The argument concerning the validity of the findings from an introspective investigation thus far has been concerned with validity in the usual sense, that is, the argument has been concerned with the truth or falsity of propositions which issue from an introspective investigation.

There is, however, a value to such propositions which is over and beyond their validity. This is their possibility rather than their truth or falsity. The knowledge that a certain dynamic is possible enhances the sensitivity of the psychological observer. To make this point concrete, let us consider the military interrogation situation. Suppose that the interrogator is interested in determining the nature of some supplies which have been moved in by the enemy. Now suppose that the prisoner being interrogated knows what these supplies are but does not wish to reveal the information. The prisoner may avail himself of the dynamic indicated by proposition 6 (the revelation of less secret secrets in order to generate the impression that he is being open and frank) and inform the interrogator at length about a great number of lesser secrets, but not the nature of the supplies. He may say, "I will tell you everything that I know, but I do not know what was in those trucks." An interrogator who was not aware of the possibility of proposition 6 might be lulled into believing the man. The interrogator might say to himself, "He is evidently telling all that he knows." On the other hand, an interrogator who is aware of the possibility of the action of the dynamic indicated by proposition 6 would be aware of the possibility of this kind of deception and would be less likely to be taken in.

If at least one person can contrive such a device for deception, then such a device is possible, and some other individual may have conceived of it and may be making use of it. The truth of the proposition in this respect becomes quite secondary. What is important, simply, is that someone thought of it; and if one person thought of it, other persons might think of it.

In this respect psychologists can make a major contribution to society not only by rendering to society established truths, but also by rendering to society established possibles with respect to psychological dynamics. In the matter of prediction and control of human behavior, a knowledge of what an individual might possibly do, or possibly feel, or possibly think, places us well on the way toward the achievement of our objective. Given a detailed knowledge concerning the possibles, we can act in such a fashion as to discourage some from becoming actualities, and to encourage others into becoming actualities. The pragmatic usefulness of knowledge of possibles extends from the clinical situation to world affairs.

As has been suggested, these possibles may indeed turn out to be truths in the larger and more scientific sense. But even if they fail to meet the criteria for general scientific propositions, they have value in the sense indicated above.

♣ ♣ ♣ ♣ ♣ ♣ ♣ ♣ ♣ ♣ *10*

Suicide
and the Method
of Introspection

As is commonly known, the method of introspection in the field of psychology went out of fashion some time ago. The last major exponent of the method of introspection was Titchener, a name which many modern psychologists would regard as the fulcrum *against* which contemporary psychology has developed. However, even the method of introspection which Titchener advocated was very far from the kind of thing which we might contemporarily associate, say, with psychoanalytic forms of introspection. It is an interesting historical fact that, although the rather barren kind of sensory introspection that Titchener advocated was decidedly rejected, a deeper, more personal kind of introspection has found its way back into the field principally through the encroaching fringe influence of psychoanalysis.

One of the paradoxes of American culture is that it has been the fertile ground upon which both behaviorism and psychoanalysis have flourished. It is beyond the scope of this paper to pursue this problem in detail. Let it be sufficient simply to point out that behaviorism and psychoanalysis have had their appeal to the strongly pragmatic current in American intellectual life. The behaviorist avowedly promised to find out enough about behavior to be able to "predict and control" it. Psychoanalysis found its way into the culture as a practical cure for ailments which were resistant to other forms of cure, and as an ideology for the cure of the larger social ailments.

But, in spite of the co-presence of these two major orientations of psychology in America, one point of the behaviorist orientation, that psychology should be of "the other one," as was so aptly expressed in one of the behavioristic pronunciamentos (Meyer, 1921), has managed to hold the field. Unofficially, there are contrary forces. In the training of clinical psychologists and psychiatrists, personal therapy might be recommended; or a supervisor might tell his student that he needs to "step into" his patient's neurosis or psychosis. But there has been very little of a systematic nature done whereby we might come to understand the nature of the introspective process in the understanding of either the "general" case or the "other one." A considerable amount of research will have to be done in order to come to an analytic understanding of what has been the domain, ostensive rather than analytic, mostly of writers of literature, largely in the romantic tradition.

This paper is then an exercise—rather than what may be considered to be a serious treatment—in the use of the method of introspection. The author is deeply aware of many of the pitfalls associated with attempting to do something which, because of a real lack of available knowledge, makes anyone at best an amateur.

The starting phenomenon taken in this exercise was the simple fact that suicide, like crime, is something extremely engaging to large numbers of people who, in all probability, will never attempt to commit suicide. What do we think of suicide? Certainly, in our culture we regard suicide as *bad*. Many of those who have taken it upon themselves to make serious investigations of the problem of suicide have characteristically shaken their heads disapprovingly as they struggled to come to an understanding of it. Our society may no longer mistreat the bodies of suicides, confiscate the property they leave, and deny them the presumptive privileges of religious rites engaged in for the sake of the dead. Yet we do moralize about suicide by commenting on the ineffectuality of the act, or on the lack of social responsibility shown by the suicide, or by "tsk"-ing about the immorality of attempting to escape from problems. Among a number of associates of the author who are involved in the clinical enterprise, there seems to be nothing which constitutes such a threat to their equanimity as the possibility or the actuality of a suicide among their patients. Although psychologists and psychiatrists have to pay large premiums (in guilt and anxiety) in connection with their clinical work, the premium associated with suicide seems to be extremely high, and perhaps excessive; and it would seem that they would like to permit themselves the outlet of outrage at a patient who has committed suicide were they not inhibited by the variety of considerations that their professional role dictates.

Suicide is a form of murder, as the etymology of the word indicates; and murder is the most heinous of crimes. Associated with murder is legal execution, the most drastic of social punishments. When a person commits suicide he participates in both of these constellations. That we should be so touched by the idea of suicide may perhaps be indicative of the fact that suicide is deeply associated with both our own murderous tendencies and our participation in the larger social act of legal execution, the deep emotion that people have felt for thousands of years as they watched a crucifixion, a beheading, or a hanging. It is perhaps more than coincidental that the major religious image of Western civilization,

115

the image of the crucifixion, is one that paradoxically contains both elements we have ascribed to the suicide—an execution, and yet one in which the very same divinity is instrumental in having made the execution come to pass.[1]

We are led by these considerations to conclude that there is a sense in which the suicidal personality, that is the personality of a person who has actually committed suicide, may actually not be grossly different from the personality of the person who has not or who will not ever make the attempt. In the course of the considerations in connection with this exercise, the author had the cooperation of a psychologist (who must perforce remain unidentified) who had actually made several serious attempts upon his own life. The relationship with this other psychologist cannot be considered to be "clinical" in the usual sense. A number of discussions were held with this psychologist concerning the meaning, etc., of the suicidal act. The methodological problem, of course, was to make the "imaginary leap." The ways in which the presumptive imaginary leap was conditioned in a biasing direction by his own personality and by his considerations of the nature of the relationship between himself and the other person must remain as possible sources of error. And whether these things are simply "difficulties" rather than "objections" we will, for now, not pursue.

In making the introspective analysis of the suicide, the author engaged in some psychotechnics, the chief of which was the attempt to bridge the gap between himself and the suicide by letting himself, on a pretense basis, be lowered into the psychological *Walpurgisnacht* of the suicide. The fact that it was a pretense has, of course, advantages and disadvantages. The chief advantage of pretense is that pretense replaces and serves the function of other defense mechanisms in the suicide. The chief disadvantage of pretense is that it is, in point of fact, pretense, and hence the question of its validity remains cogent. Methodologically, this imaginary leap can be regarded as the serious entertainment of the contrary-to-fact conditional, a method which is perhaps central to effective

[1] See Freud's analysis of the meaning of the crucifixion in *Moses and Monotheism* (1955).

scientific work; for to say that A causes B involves at least a consideration of the consequences of not-A. To help the imaginary leap the author read considerably in the literature on suicide, the objective in the reading always being that of attempting to absorb the mood, the feeling tone, of the suicidal personality. The author also went back over his notes of a suicidal case he had worked with, and the notes of other psychologists and psychiatrists on several suicidal patients. Still another psychotechnical device that the author used, one which is logically partly derivative from the other devices, may be called the "negation" technique. The basic idea behind this method is Freud's (1950), that although in consciousness we appreciate the meaning of "not," the unconscious does not understand the meaning of this word. Thus, if the author could bring himself to introspect on the living, he might also be brought to a point where he might betray to his conscious self what goes on with respect to dying. As is evident from the necessity of having to resort to such a device, the internal resistances with respect to the active entertainment of the idea of suicide are quite strong. In the course of work on this problem a number of the resistances were made manifest, but what remained can, of course, not be said.

Thus, ask "Why live?" instead of "Why commit suicide?" We take it for granted that life should be a continuous, self-sustaining process, and that it is natural for it to be that way. We do not ordinarily challenge the basic value-premise that life is good; and we feel that it is a basic denial of all of our other values to deny the value of life itself. Furthermore, the act of suicide is an act which calls for a high marshaling of the volitional processes; lacking that, and lacking other cause of death, we will continue to endure into the next moment.

Then, living, in the social sense, maintains life. When one drives a car on the highway, one assumes that the other driver will continue to stay alive until his car has passed. The tremendous amount of dependence of people upon one another is based upon their continuity as living. We simply assume that the "other" person, upon whom we depend, will continue to live, and, as we know from the clinical experience with children, a parent who has died

117

is attributed with having wanted to leave. Thus, there is a very important sense in which living is a social obligation. And suicide must be ether actually, or at least symbolically, a defection in social obligation. The fact that suicide is regarded as a crime, putting it into the class of other forms of social defection, may then not be without point.

Living seems to entail a sense of openness of the durational dimension. One wants to continue to live in order to "be around later." This is in rather dramatic contrast to the suicide. For the suicide the sense of duration is somehow blocked off. An important distinction needs, however, to be made. It is not that there is something necessarily wrong with the cognitive processes of the suicide. It is not that he does not appreciate the continuity and the passage of time cognitively—there is even some reason to believe that this cognitive appreciation is enhanced. But the sense of time as the matrix of possibility seems to be stultified. In nonsuicidal living, if we can use such a term, the future is the container, in the phenomenological framework, of possibility. In the imaginary leap the author picked up the feeling of being "blocked," as in a game of chess in which every move that one thinks of making is blocked; and although it was not phenomenologically like boredom, it was similar to boredom in the sense in which, in the state of boredom, everything that one thinks of to do has no appeal. Perhaps one of the things about the future which is lacking in the suicide is the hope and excitement of the unrevealed, the sense of the possibility of deep gratification.

The personality of the suicide, as has been pointed out many times, is one saturated with aggression, as though the liquid of aggression had been poured over every thought, feeling, and wish. But over and beyond this pervasive aggressive atmosphere, there seems to be a prototypic role, interiorized in the personality of the suicide, against which the act of aggression is turned. This role is best characterized by the term the "caretaker." Somehow, it seems that the caretaker is much more diffuse than something we can ascribe to any person. I am tempted to say that in the act of suicide the person is aggressing against the mother, for the mother is the

118

person who has kept the individual alive, who has taken him out of the danger of infantile impotence, and who "took care" of maintaining life until the individual was able to "take care" of himself. There is a sense in which the act of suicide is the undoing of the mother. Yet, although this may be true in part, it would seem that the caretaker is much more general and much more diffuse than can be ascribed to any person in the infantile family constellation. It is as though the individual who commits suicide is so bound by the caretaking function in the fulfillment of his wishes that he would rather slay the caretaker in himself than live the life of bondage to the caretaker. It would seem that the act of suicide is a spiteful act—whatever the psychodynamics of spite may be—against the tyrannical caretaker. In several of the cases to which the author exposed himself, he was able to pick up a sense of the subjects suffering the feeling of not being taken care of. The act of suicide is a single act, albeit a paradoxical one, in which the individual "takes care" of himself.

One of the most interesting features of the act of suicide, especially in the instances where the attempt is successful, is the exceedingly high degree of managerial, executive quality which is manifested. There is great foresight with respect to the contingencies, including the contingency of "weakening." It has all of the characteristics of "good" caretaking, with the exception of the manifest objective. It is less than flippancy to point out that the words "execute" and "executive" can settle with accuracy upon the act of suicide. The high competence which the very act of suicide calls for, and which is manifested in the successful suicidal act, combined with the fact that the act of suicide is self-destructive, suggests what we may call a paradox of individualism in the suicide. For, on the one hand, the act of suicide is an act which must be conceived and planned and carried out on the basis of one's own initiative, without consultation with anyone else, and without anyone else's cooperation or moral support, and sometimes over the obstacles that others might place in one's path. It is an act which involves an independence of enterprise and an alienation from others extremely rare in our otherwise cooperative society. It

119

is highly private, self-determined. Yet, it is enmeshed in the whole nexus of interrelationships that the person has with others, especially focused about his dependency upon others.

One can suppose that the suicidal personality is one in which there is thus a gross imbalance in the self-other relationships. If we can accept the idea that the suicidal person is one who feels that there is something wanting in his caretaking, and who, only with a great marshaling of energy, can exert himself in his own caretaking, it would seem that the immediate precondition of the act of suicide is an accentuation of the sense of not-being-taken-care-of which calls forth a grand burst of I-will-take-care-of-myself energies as compensatory. The conflict is that of wanting on the one hand to surrender one's individuality in exchange for succor, and that of a strenuous denial of dependency. The suicide draws the curtain with a burst of individualistic energies, feeling that he could not sustain this for long, but that he can manage to be thus highly individualistic for the short space of time that the climax of the suicidal act calls for.

In the consideration of the personality of the suicide, the term conforming psychopathic personality repeatedly suggested itself. Considering the usual sense of the terms "conforming" and "psychopathic personality," putting them together appears as a contradiction in terms. Yet the suicide seems to be such that both terms apply. For, in his ordinary presuicidal functioning, the suicide seems to conform; and, somehow, he is in the hope that by proper conforming he might possibly win a psychological income that will provide him with a "living." At the same time, there are features of the personality of the suicide which make the term "psychopath" apt. For, primarily, there is an ability to set aside, in the suicidal act itself, the action of the superego. The ability to carry out a murder is present, even if the murdered person is the person himself. At the beginning of this paper, we referred to the incipient sense of outrage the suicide produces in psychologists and psychiatrists who have worked with him, and the classical patterns of outrage against the suicide we have seen historically. It is this same kind of outrage that the psychopath produces in us. For we react negatively to the psychopath because he permits himself things which most normals have gone to a great expense to deny themselves. Whereas the outrage can bring itself to expression in connection with the psychopath, the suicide manages to cheat us of this opportunity by imposing upon himself the ultimate punishment, death. He perplexes us by his both allowing expression to his antisocial impulses and eliciting from us our pity.

▲▲▲▲▲▲▲▲▲▲▲ *11*

Psychotherapist:
Healer or Repairman?

One of the major professional problems in the field of psychology is that of role definition. This problem is most acute in psychotherapy. Morality in psychotherapy is part of this larger problem. I have sometimes thought that nondirective therapy, aside from its intrinsic values, appeals to some psychologists because it makes a firm role commitment unnecessary in the course of psychotherapy.

There are certain classical roles—teacher, priest, lawyer, physician—which are interpersonally intimate. Psychotherapists have drawn heavily upon these role models. But none of them have fit satisfactorily.

One role model which has arisen recently is worthy of some attention because of its popularity among psychologist-psychotherapists. It is that of *scientist*—discoverer, researcher, writer and reader of technical papers, studied unbeliever in the undemonstrated, and arrogant believer in self-effacement. This role has become important professionally because the major reference roles have usually been *teacher* and *physician*. For the former, the role of scientist is an enhancement; for the latter, it has been a lever to place the psychologist-psychotherapist at an advantage. Let me not depreciate this role; it has its value. But it need not be used to screen and protect the psychotherapist. The psychologist-psychotherapist role has its own intrinsic value and need not come in on the coattails of the scientist. I hope there will always be psychotherapists who are also research workers. But the value of the psychotherapeutic enterprise need not be contingent upon the value of the research enterprise.

If the real issues are not to be evaded the psychologist has available to him two main role postures, *repairman* and *healer*.

Let us consider first the role of repairman. It is familiar enough in contemporary times. When it is not corrupt and vulgar, the role posture is self-effacing, polite, formal, pleasant. Technical competence dominates all other aspects of personality. Everything is subservient to competence. The repairman interests himself in matters of fact. He has license to investigate as thoroughly as the situation demands. He is both without squeamishness and without intrusiveness. He gets little pleasure from his work except the pleasure from a job well done. His craftsman's intelligence proceeds systematically, orderly, efficiently, parsimoniously, economically. He restores to order whatever he puts out of order in the course of his work. It is not without respect that I present this image of the repairman. One cannot be a citizen of the contemporary world without valuing this role posture as an ideal. There are many instances in which this role posture is both possible and appropriate. Indeed, where it is appropriate, it would be wonderful if our psychotherapists could come close to this ideal. But before it can be said that the role posture of repairman is appropriate, the objectives must be clear and unambiguous.

The existence of clear and unambiguous objectives is the major criterion for the appropriateness of the repairman role. In psychotherapy there can be no clear and unambiguous predecisions concerning man's thoughts, feelings, and wishes. Man's objectives for the kind of being he wishes to be are the intrinsically unfinished business of his life. Some psychologists, at least since Watson's time, have boasted that they could produce any kind of a human being one might specify. I do not grant them their boast. The state of the art is not yet so refined. But even were that boast granted, the rub is that they could produce intelligence only after specifications were provided. There is precious little to offer from psychological research by which to make specifications for mankind. The adventure in his human existence is, I think, intrinsic to the nature of man.

Consider now the role posture of the healer. First, let me say I am not advocating a historical regression to suggestion, charlatanry, hocus-pocus, vulgar religiosity. I am not advocating the replacement of competence with charisma. I am not advocating the exertion of the force of the personality of the psychotherapist as a psychotherapeutic agency. Rather, we must be aware that deeply embedded in our culture are certain needs, social forms, expectations, and the like, which are responded to by certain roles. These are abiding forms in the culture, and they are but little modified by the changes of the world to which we are witness. Presumptive role innovations draw upon classical models and function in the same way as they do.

The healer is a personage who abides in Western civilization. For almost two thousand years the most abiding personage has been Jesus, who was a healer and who has been much imitated. Characteristically the healer is religiously involved, but often outside of the pale of formal religious institutions. He is sometimes maligned, sometimes worshipped, sometimes the object of curiosity, and sometimes even the object of scientific investigation. The role has been ubiquitous. I think that it has been greatly drawn upon by psychotherapists. And I think that it has continuing value for psychotherapists. I believe that the role is supported by the properties of man, that it is an expression of the properties of man, and that it is intimately connected with the special circumstances of man's existence on this planet.

Let me characterize the major features of the healer role as I see them.

First, the healer manages, in one way or another, to inform the "client" that his suffering is not necessarily tied to his sins. The healer has his place in a world which takes suffering as the correlate of sin. The healer has his place as the expression of the other pole in the dialectic, in which the one pole is that suffering and sin are correlated. The healer denies this correlation and communicates the denial. The ways of denying the correlation of suffering and sin are multiple; and there are both religio-mystical and secular ways. The healer may take the sins upon himself, point out that Jesus takes the sins upon himself, locate the evil in alien spirits which have taken unwarranted occupancy in the body or soul. The healer may stress God's mercy, which acts as a depressor variable on the correlation of sin and suffering. More secularly, the healer may assert a deterministic metaphysics which denies responsibility, assert that the suffering is the result of infantile and, hence, innocent experiences, locate the root of the suffering in the unconscious, and the like. These are latter-day forms for depressing the correlation of suffering and sin.

Second, the healer makes the assumption that the forces for the healing are inherent in the sufferer. The healer's role is simply that of encouraging these forces to become effective. The illness of the client is understood as the interference with these powers. As contrasted with the repairman, the healer's agency is not to supply the efficient cause, but only to permit the pre-existing forces in the client to function.

Third, the healer cognizes and indicates the cosmological and existential entailment in the suffering. He points out the meaning of the individual's life in regions which extend far beyond the limited circumscribed world of the client's everyday consciousness;

125

and he thereby enhances and gives moment to the individual's existence.

Fourth, the major device the healer uses is communication. His major role is that of enhancing communication among regions of existence, whether this be between the holy and the mundane, between one person and another, between consciousness and unconsciousness, or between the scientist and the layman.

I am sure that it is evident that these characteristics I have indicated as descriptive of the healer role are already involved in good psychotherapy today. The metaphors may vary, but the basic semantic content is the same in modern times. It is, of course, important that messages be transmitted in language which is itself not offensive to the modern mind. It should also be evident that what we are saying here about the healer role posture (and the repairman, for that matter) are not scientific propositions to be evaluated in terms of "true" or "false." Rather the suggestion made here is a strategy, which I think might have some very useful outcomes. And, as I have already indicated, the field of psychotherapy has not been loath to actually avail itself of this strategy.

I cannot end this discussion without indicating two major obstacles that the healer role posture must encounter and deal with: magic on the one hand and rigid scientism on the other. As a healer, one concerns oneself with things that are only limitedly comprehended. Success in these areas makes one feel like a magician. (Freud said this of himself when he began with the cure of certain cases of hysteria.) This is a temptation to be avoided by the healer. A healer should believe in the abiding mystery of what he concerns himself with, but a magician must never believe in "magic" in the mysterious sense. The magician becomes a failure if he believes the illusions that he creates. A rigid scientism, on the other hand, is so impatient with anything short of well-founded belief that it closes off from consideration the realities which have not yet been encompassed by science. Both of these are to be avoided.

A Perspective
on
Psychoanalytic Theory

In attempting to place psychoanalytic theory in perspective, I assume that the beginning of all of our intellectual enterprises is some original condition of wonder which can be expressed in the question "What is this all about, anyhow?" We are uneasy about our experiences, and our intellectual enterprises constitute our efforts to interpret them. In the social sciences our wonder is directed at people, always with the awareness, sometimes more and sometimes less clear, that the wonderer himself is one of those people.

127

To appreciate the contribution of Freud to the intellectual fabric of our culture, let us consider rather briefly a few of the major contributors to the self-definition of man. Durkheim has shown how an act, which on the face of it appears to entail the most private decision that anyone can possibly make—committing suicide—is a socially determined event. Weber has shown how so conspicuously secular and nonreligious an activity as making money is the result of the long reach out of the religious history of mankind into the present. John Stuart Mill painstakingly sought to demonstrate and to protect man's elbow room in spite of his commitment to living with and deferring to others. In Freud's writings there is an image of man which is so intimately personal that it forces us to see how man, in his interaction with others, forces himself to forget that intimately personal, that is, to engage in repression.

When anyone attempts to describe what man is, he is involved with saying what man ought to be. To put this a bit more technically, it is that the descriptive is never free from the normative. More classically, it is the deep intrinsic relationship between the true and the good.

Consider John Locke. Basically he was an equalitarian. His image of man was that of a *tabula rasa,* a "scientific" version of normative equality, since, if men are born as blank slates, they are born equal.

An early anthropologist in the nineteenth century, who wrote when a certain romanticism was more current, said that man may be distinguished from other animals by his being able to gain from experience, to express his ideas, to sense beauty, and to look into and care for the future (Waitz, 1863). But a few decades later, when industrialization had become an important fact of human existence, another anthropologist said, "Man may be differentiated from all other animals by the fact that he is a skilled mechanic" (Munro, 1909). When mankind is involved in pressing for an equalitarian position, everyone is born as a *tabula rasa:* and when skilled mechanics are needed, men are conceived of as mechanics.

128

We need not, however, be cynical about our knowledge of man. Rather, our scientific work is part and parcel of our total impulse to interpret our experiences for ourselves in ways which are meaningful to us. It is rather that the normative in man is what sensitizes him to perceive this or that and makes him conceive of himself in one way or another.

Indeed, I would like to offer my own conception of the nature of man. This is that man is the self-fashioning being. Man is the only animal who can make himself into what he wants to be. He can learn and grow in self-determined directions. Technology and modern democratic arrangements are increasing the self-fashioning potentiality in mankind.

In a world in which man fashions himself, we have a plethora of normative-descriptive options. The competition in the social sciences is less a competition among ideas in terms of their validity than among norms for man on how he is to be. The recent pluralistic development of the social sciences itself emerges out of man's ability to fashion himself.

Consider psychoanalysis. It is distinguished from other social sciences in that its starting point is the modification of human beings, therapy. It grew to a theory of personality and to a total viewpoint, reaching into biology, history, religion, child rearing, education, and so forth. Freud started with the neurotic patients who came to him and said, in effect, that they did not like the way they were and that they wanted help in becoming different. If you allow that man is a self-fashioning being, then psychoanalysis comes in to deal with man in articulation with his self-fashioning potentiality.

The creation and the acceptance of psychoanalysis were in response to the experience of alienation that has been associated with urbanization. The type of human being centrally represented in the psychoanalytical literature is that of a person who is "maladjusted" to the demands of life, who is already alienated at least in the sense that a smooth relationship between him and the external world does not prevail. He is a person in whom the control over himself has balked in the face of demands upon him. The neurosis is a state of affairs in which the individual finds himself responding differently to demands as interpreted by the ego.

Freud, the originator of psychoanalysis, was a profoundly alienated Jew living in the city of Vienna. He started his career as a neurophysiological research worker, and appears to have been separated from his laboratory position because he was Jewish. He was deeply alienated from medical circles and regretted his medical background and identification. He was alienated from academic circles and wrote bitterly over the lack of recognition that he received. He was cognizant of the relationship between his alienation as a Jew and his advocacy of psychoanalysis, saying: "Nor is it perhaps entirely a matter of chance that the first advocate of psychoanalysis was a Jew. To profess belief in this new theory called for a certain degree of readiness to accept a position of solitary opposition—a position with which no one is more familiar than a Jew" (Freud, 1952). Practically all of the early psychoanalysts were urban Jews; and a recent study of the practice of psychiatry in New Haven has shown that about 80 per cent of the practicing psychoanalysts are Jews (Redlich and Hollingshead, 1958).

The relationship between psychoanalysis and alienation is also patent when we consider the kind of acceptance psychoanalysis has had in the United States. It has had little association with the political, social, and economic centers of power and influence in our society. Its acceptance by medicine has been belated and begrudging; and the actual practice of psychoanalysis has been restricted to small numbers in major urban areas. It has had mostly negative acceptance in American academic institutions, and little even of that.

Where psychoanalysis has had its major influence, and there it has been of great magnitude, is among the independent artists and writers, largely urban, the group which is perhaps one of the most alienated in American culture. One historian of American literature (Cargill, 1941) writes:

Of the ideologists influential in America, the most important, of course, was Sigmund Freud, whose visit in 1909 literally caused an earthquake in public opinion. Mark Sullivan in *Our Times*

130

records that after 1910 the newspapers were packed with references to Freud's doctrines and that in the next decade more than two hundred books were written on Freudianism. The reaction of the mature American was horror; consequently the immature generation in revolt against its elders took up the banner of Freud. He became their "philosopher," for, as Thomas Mann insists, Freud is more important as a thinker than as a scientist, and certainly this is true so far as his influence in America is concerned.

Let us consider the following items of psychoanalytic thought: repression, sexuality, the view of man as metaphorically expressive, and development.

1. *Repression.* Repression is perhaps one of the earliest notions Freud developed and a keystone of psychoanalysis. It is the process by which things are "put out of mind." Repression is not always pathological. The general experience we so often have in the normal conduct of life when we say, "I would rather not think about that now," is a normal prototype of repression. This mechanism, however, in an exaggerated form, is the root of neurosis. The psychoanalyst takes as his prime treatment objective the overcoming of the work of the repressive mechanism.

In somewhat oversimplified terms, the message of psychoanalysis is that we repress into a psychological subterranean life many of the thoughts, feelings, and wishes which are profoundly important to us but which fail to meet the criteria of normality, propriety, deference, conformity, consensus, effectiveness, and physical survival, criteria understood by the psychoanalyst as being associated with the ego, and that part of it called the superego.

The repressive mechanism is highly subject to forces which are conspicuously cultural. A good deal of the attention of psychoanalysis was directed to those factors, particularly those affecting the child at a very early age, which were culturally lodged and which could be identified within the family. One of the important sets of such factors is that associated with the Protestant ethic. Orderliness, methodicalness, self-control, industriousness, single-minded guidance of behavior in terms of preset goals, avoiding the

131

temptations to sloth associated with gregariousness and affection, are all values associated with the Protestant ethic. The Protestant ethic may be understood as a vaulting expression of the normal ego and superego functions in mankind. This frame of mind was associated with the development of urban-industrial society.

We are now in a somewhat better position to understand the appeal of psychoanalysis to the artistic and literary segment of our society. Art and literature have often represented rebellion against the Protestant ethic. The overcoming of repression imposed by this ethic has been one of the major links of the artist and the writer to psychoanalysis. This is made clear in a book by Norman Brown (1959) in which, among other things, Brown says that with Protestantism the death instinct became the master of the house, alluding to the identification made by Freud between the death instinct and the forces associated with the ego and the superego. In addition, the artist and writer saw in psychoanalysis a touchstone for the overcoming of the internal resistances to creativity, with, for example, Gertrude Stein having been specifically influenced in her free associative writing by the work of Freud.

The artist and writer are not clearly "gainfully employed." Their products have little conspicuous utility, and for the most of them there is only a remote connection between their work and the making of money. Their work, to them expressive, is, from the point of view of the Protestant ethic, self-indulgent. Their emphasis on human emotion is an emphasis on human weakness. The preoccupation of the romantic writer with the "natural" condition of mankind is effeminate. The bohemian life of the artist is "morally depraved." Indeed, the conflict between the bohemian and the bourgeois, one of the deepest conflicts within our society, is the conflict between those who are opposed to and those who are in favor of the Protestant ethic.

The very practice of psychoanalysis itself can be regarded as the height of sloth, self-indulgence, and improvidence: lying on a couch for an hour in the middle of the day, five days a week for several years, talking about anything that comes to mind, especially yourself, in a disorganized fashion, profoundly unclear about what

132

you may be accomplishing, and paying money to someone to listen to you! The Protestant ethic could justify the psychoanalyst, for he watches the clock and makes money, but not the patient, unless the patient can rationalize it as an investment, investment being an acceptable notion within the Protestant ethic.

Let us return to the matter of alienation. It is essentially a condition in which the ego is not functioning effectively in its relationship to the outside world. Put in very simple terms, the person needs either to get into himself or to get out of himself; more technically, to enter into the deeper reaches of the psyche, or to re-energize the ego functions in connection with the outside world with a vaulting effort to master it. The first strategy entails the reduction of the repression, the second its enhancement. In more recent urban-industrial civilization, the power of the single individual to modify the world on his own tended to decrease, and at least one response to this was to regard the notions of psychoanalysis with favor, as providing a way by which an inward turn was made more possible. By pointing out that there was an important region in the psyche which was unconscious, the Freudian way of thinking provided an invitation of making conscious what was unconscious. This is the meaning of that oft-quoted phrase by Freud, "Where id was, there shall ego be." The id, which was unconscious, should be made conscious. The forces of repression should be weakened. The boundary of the ego should be enlarged to include material which had been repressed. The strategy associated with psychoanalytic thought is to encourage the individual to enter into the regions which were closed by repression so that he can re-emerge from it more adequate to the life that he wants to live. In the words of one psychoanalyst, Ernst Kris (1952), it is to encourage "regression in the service of the ego."

The psychoanalytic vision tended to encourage a concept of mankind far richer than the highly instrumentalized one of the Protestant ethic and the associated urban-industrial society. The meaning of life had been converted into work and, more crassly, into the amount of money one could accumulate. Parenthetically, in Marx, the value of work is maintained, but it is separated from

133

the making of money in the sense of the Protestant ethic. The meaning of persons to each other largely became their significance as customers and workers. The Protestant ethic was associated with a deep distrust among people, a reluctance to confide in one another, and a "deep spiritual isolation," as Weber pointed out. The fundamental roles allowed for interpersonal relations were largely in terms of the market—the commodities market or the labor market—creating what Erich Fromm has referred to as the "marketplace mentality." What was given by psychoanalysis was an image of the person far richer and more complicated and more personal than that of any other prevailing set of ideas on the nature of mankind. Work and its associated psychological mechanism, repression, had depersonalized mankind. And psychoanalysis, with its ideal of overcoming repression, seemed to rescue mankind from this depersonalization.

2. *Sexuality*. Psychoanalysis stressed the significance of sexuality as characterizing the psyche in its depths. With the growth of urban-industrial society, the notion of puritanism became associated with the repression of the sexual and devotion to work. One of the important concomitants of the Protestant ethic and the urban-industrial revolution was the change in the value of children. At least from the seventeenth century, the intimate bonds of care and education of children began to break up. Such things as the sale of children to masters took place; and law after law had to be passed to force these masters to care for their charges (Bailyn, 1960). The abuses of children and their neglect, so effectively drawn in fiction by Charles Dickens, had been an abiding reality since the beginning of the industrial revolution. In the United States, in the late nineteenth and early twentieth centuries, having children was regarded as slothful and the mark of the lower classes. "The rich grow richer, and the poor have children!" it was said. In the early part of the twentieth century, there was a great deal of writing devoted to what appeared as the disaster of America, that the genetic stock was going to degenerate because of the high birth rate among the poor and the low birth rate among the rich. In general, all of this entailed a belief in the inverse relationship

between family, children, and sexuality, on the one hand, and the achievement of the values associated with the urban-industrial society, on the other.

Thus psychoanalysis, with its emphasis on sexuality, appeared as antipuritanical. Not that it advocated wantonness. It did, however, make sexuality a conscious concern. Psychoanalysis stressed the sexual in adults and infants, and in the relations of children to parents. Freud's famous formula for the essential values of life was *"Arbeit und Liebe,"* work and love, rather than work instead of love, which had developed as a fundamental ideal of the Protestant ethic.

Freud took sexuality as the touchstone of all of life. At least one contemporary psychoanalyst, Erikson (1963) has been able to interpret this for the appreciation of the relationships of various factors in human personality to society at large. Freud's notion of the Oedipus complex indicates that the central problem of man is in his relationship to his parents, and that this relationship is profoundly sexual in nature. The notion highlights the fact that the critical question in the life of the psyche is related to its personal existence, existence which results from the very banal fact that sexuality and reproduction are closely related. What is dramatically indicated in the notion of the Oedipus complex is that the fundamental biological linkage of human beings to one another is one of the principal forces which become repressed in the course of the life of the individual.

3. *Metaphor.* A metaphor is a figure of speech which is not literally true, used to communicate something not literally said. What emerges from such a work as *The Interpretation of Dreams* is the degree to which the normal psychological functioning of the human being involves the making and using of metaphor. In the ordinary use of metaphor, the object of the construction is the enhancement of communication. What we learn from Freud is that metaphor is also used to conceal meaning, and that it is the way by which the individual allows psychological fulfilment of the wish in ways which he does not himself recognize. Freud's *The Interpretation of Dreams* is essentially an essay on the way metaphors

are created, offering such concepts as condensation and displacement by which to understand them; and on how to find the hidden meaning by sidetracking the repressive mechanism.

Freud would lead us to understand that the repressive mechanism makes for literalism; and that the overcoming of repression is at the same time the appreciation of the meaning of metaphor. *The Interpretation of Dreams* can be taken as criticism of the literalism which is associated with both the life of the ego and the methodical demands of the urban-industrial society. In both of these the literalism tends to eschew the metaphorical. The dream is a prototype of what the literal mind says is not true of the world. It is like hallucination and delusion. In the literal sense what happens in the dream is false. But what we come to understand as we read through *The Interpretation of Dreams* is the sense in which truth is entailed in it. Through the understanding of the dream we come to what Freud referred to as "the essence of our being." The major way by which we come to this is to appreciate that the dream is metaphorical of a deeper psychological reality, the kind of reality which is blown away upon awakening and entering into the daytime literal world of the ego.

4. *Development.* To understand the psychoanalytic view of human development, we contrast it to the view associated with classical English philosophy: that development is the increase of knowledge through the informative senses—the eyes and ears, primarily, and, to a lesser degree, taste, smell, and touch.

In contrast, Freud stressed the noninformative sensations from the oral, anal, and genital regions of the body. In Freudian thought the significance of the informative senses is principally associated with the functioning of the ego and relates to the fact that the human being is materially separated from his environment. The informative senses principally inform the musculature and are related to the free movement of the individual in space. The oral, anal, and genital regions are related to the ingress and egress of the material substances associated with the actual physical existence of the being and the material production of other beings. These regions involve much more intimate functions than, say, the eyes and the ears. The latter inform about the remote, and their functioning is based on the separateness of the individual from the environment. The oral, anal, and genital entail the continuity of the human being with the rest of the physical world and other people. The informative senses are the ones related to alienation. The separate physical existence of the person is an outstanding fact to the ego. Not that the Freudian point of view does not show how the separate ego emerges. But what it does show is that there is a significant place in the psyche for the psychological counterpart of the physical continuity of persons with one another, expressed most sharply in sexual yearning, and biologically centered on those parts of the body most materially continuous with the rest of the world.

It is not only the material continuity with the rest of the world but also with the temporal continuity that the psychoanalytic position stressed. The romantic had indicated that the child is father of the man, as Wordsworth put it. Freud added cogent details about the relationship of childhood to adulthood.

The classical theory of development is essentially interested only in the life of the ego. It appears to accept the condition of alienation and tries to make the most out of it. It is not at all irrelevant to point out that this English philosophy emerged together with the development of the Protestant ethic in society and with the development of our urban-industrial society. The psychoanalytic point of view, on the other hand, starts with an uneasiness with the life of the ego and with alienation and seeks to find within the psyche those things which precede, and are beyond, the limited life of the ego, stressing always the continuity of the life of the individual with the rest of the world and other people, past and present and future.

Let me close with a brief word or two about each of these four major items in connection with the notion of man as a self-fashioning being.

Repression: This notion goes together with the conviction that through the turn inward, which is involved in overcoming repression, the person is brought to a point where he can cope better with the external. Freud discovered the paradox that the

137

turn inward toward self-understanding entails greater outward effectiveness.

Sexuality: Freud's emphasis on sexuality is essentially an emphasis on the deepest existential core of the personality, and an emphasis on the necessity of consciously apprehending this existential core.

Metaphor: Freud recognized that man often expresses himself concerning his deeper existential problems in metaphor; and that, in order to modify himself, man must become alert to the meanings metaphorically carried by his own expressions.

And, finally, *development:* Development at root involves the continuity of the individual with the rest of the world. In the breaks of this continuity is development arrested; and it is facilitated by the restoration of the conditions associated with this continuity.

♣ ♣ ♣ ♣ ♣ ♣ ♣ ♣ ♣ ♣ ♣ ♣ ♣ *13*

Science, Mysticism,
and
Psychoanalysis

Consider the three modes of thought: science, mysticism, and psychoanalysis. In our usual thinking there is a polarity with science at one end, and mysticism at the other. But there may be an error in this polarity, and the consideration of psychoanalysis as somehow being both and neither may help us to see the error in it.

Silvan Tomkins (1964) has made the extremely valuable observation that among mathematicians there are those of the "right" and those of the "left," those who are attracted to mathematics because of its seeming certainty and discipline (the right-ists), and those who are attracted because mathematics has novelty, the promise of excitement, and admission into wild and unaccount-able spaces (the leftists). This is a valuable distinction, and I think it can be used with profit for all modes of thought. I submit that there probably are scientists, mystics, and psychoanalysts of both the right and the left. I also think that the innovators are more likely to be of the left than the right in each instance. And, I think, the only genuine polarity between science and mysticism is between that of scientists of the right and mystics of the left. When we consider both scientists and mystics of the left, the distinction between them tends to fade.

Let us be somewhat empirical. Indeed, one of the major objections that can be made against those who have written on the scientific approach to psychology is that they are characteristically not very empirical. The common rhetorical form "science is this" and "science is that" is hardly ever backed up with empirical ob-servations on the scientific enterprise itself. When one actually *looks* at the history of science, and examines the people who have been the major figures in that history, one repeatedly comes across such people as Newton, Kepler, Pascal—and Fechner in psy-chology—who were profoundly mystical in their orientation. And in modern times there are people like Einstein, Schrödinger, Planck, Whitehead, Eddington, Jeans, Wittgenstein, and others in whom there are identifiable mystical streaks by any reasonable definition of the term. Reading such books as Burtt's *The Metaphysical Foundations of Modern Physical Science* (1954) and Bertrand Russell's *Mysticism and Logic* (1953) seriously suggests the possi-bility that the mystical orientation is more than mere idiosyncrasy among leading figures in the history of science.

I would like to comment parenthetically on the myth of the ineptitude of mystics, and again take a somewhat empirical orientation. Einstein was hardly inept when he wrote the letter to Roosevelt which led to the release of nuclear energy; and the ideas of the mystical Isaac Newton have played most significant roles in the revolutionary changes of the face of the earth of the last few

140

hundred years. David McClelland's studies of achievement and the achievement motive are relevant, for he suggests (1961), on the basis of his observations, that one major source of achievement motivation is "positive mysticism." He observes the remarkable business success of the Quakers in the United States, the Jains, the Vaishnava Hindus, and the Parsees of India, and the Japanese military caste, the samurai, who are associated with Zen Buddhism (which, parenthetically, is having a wave of success in success-oriented United States). We can also add to this the success of the Americans who took to transcendentalism and the wealthy Christian Science movement. Nor is it completely inappropriate to point out that the psychoanalytic movement, which has deep roots in Jewish mysticism (Bakan, 1958), is one of the few psychologies which seems to hold out real promise in connection with mental health; and that the practitioners in this school of thought are not in poverty. One may also cite in this connection the data gathered by Sorokin (1950) on the longevity of saints which can be used to support a thesis that those given to a mystical orientation tend to live longer than others.

Let me explicate some important identities among the three modes of thought I have mentioned. These identities in the language of the mystic are the "one," the "beyond," and meditation. Although the language and the general rhetoric may be different in science and psychoanalysis, the beliefs associated with "one," "beyond," and meditation are essential to science, mysticism, and psychoanalysis.

Briefly, these three beliefs are as follows:

1. The notion of the "one" entails a belief in a fundamental unity in spite of apparent disunity.
2. "Beyond" entails a belief in the distinction between what is manifest and what is not manifest, and the conviction that what is not manifest influences what is manifest.
3. The emphasis on meditation entails the conviction that through some kind of intrapsychic activity one can come into contact with what is not manifest.

141

Let us first consider the idea of unity, the "one." According to Bertrand Russell (1953) the "refusal to admit opposition or division anywhere" is an essential characteristic of mysticism. In making this point he cites Heraclitus' assertion that good and evil are one. The coalescence of mysticism, psychoanalysis, and science is clearly evident in connection with the matter of good and evil. In the thought of many religious mystics the distinction between good and evil is dissolved. For God had created the world, and apparent evil could not really be evil, but behind both good and evil there is a singular unity. It is equally the case that in the scientific enterprise the distinction between good and evil tends to vanish. In psychoanalytic treatment we also allow these categories to dissolve into one another. Certainly there is evil in man, but we do not allow ourselves in the treatment of the mentally disturbed to reject them from our egos. Rather we seek to discover those underlying conditions in all human beings which are singular, and see good and evil as derivative and apparent, allowing ourselves to work with this underlying reality for which the words "good" and "evil" are irrelevant, and also ascertaining what is the case and what really goes on. Psychoanalysis is particularly important, for it has given us some insight into the very mechanisms whereby we make the judgment of good and evil, and it has taught us some of the ways whereby we can make use in our very functioning of this penchant we have for making such judgments.

It may also be observed that the scientist refuses to cognize any basic disunity even more generally in connection with his knowledge. The conviction of a basic unity behind apparent disunity has been the key theme of the "unity of science" movement of modern times. In the clinical situation the lack of unity and integration in the individual has often been taken as the essential feature of psychological difficulty; and the clinical program has characteristically had the achievement of unity in the personality as its aim.

It is one of the most notable contributions of the psychoanalytic movement to have been able to recognize fundamental unities behind apparent disunities. Consider, for example, Freud's paper on demoniacal possession (1950). In it he comments:

> It requires no great analytic insight to divine that God and the Devil were originally one and the same, a single figure which was later split into two bearing opposite characteristics. . . .
> It is an example of a process so familiar to us, by which an idea with an opposed—ambivalent—content is split into two opposites contrasting sharply. The antitheses contained in the original idea of the nature of God are but a reflection of the ambivalence governing the relation of an individual to his personal father. . . . The father is thus the individual prototype of both God and the Devil [pp. 450–451].

There is, of course, the danger of falling into an obscurantism, the kind of obscurantism which wallows in paradoxes and contradictions and rests content in seeming profundity without advancing clarity. And it is certainly the case that sometimes both mysticism and psychoanalysis fall into the error of obscurantism, in asserting essential unity. Consider the fundamental and abstract disunity A and not-A. No matter how much we might object to the simplicism of Aristotelian logic, nonetheless A, and its negation, not-A, cannot both be true. But it is here that psychoanalysis helps us to understand. It was through the analysis of the role of negation that Freud was able to come upon some underlying truths about the nature of the human psyche which in themselves help us to understand the nature of the negation itself.

In Freud's paper on negation, he indicates that the function of negation is to aid in the overcoming of repression. "By the help of the symbol of negation, the thinking-process frees itself from the limitations of repression and enriches itself with the subject-matter without which it could not work efficiently" (Freud, 1952).

The negation makes it possible to admit things to consideration at least in some way, without rejecting these things completely. Negation is a device whereby the regions of what may be considered are opened more widely. The best example of this that we can bring forth in this context is the *un*conscious itself, that is, the negation of the conscious. How may we think of the unconscious except by thinking of it as the negation of the conscious? For it is only the conscious which is perceptible. As Freud says in this paper: "There is no stronger evidence that we have been successful in uncovering the unconscious than when the patient reacts with the words 'I didn't think that' or 'I never thought of that.' " This is not a wallowing in contradiction. This is the use of negation, and the proper use of negation is based on the more fundamental assumption that under all negation must lie a unity.

But now let us think of science again. In the proper pursuit of the scientific enterprise there is always the pursuit of negation. We seek counterevidence to our propositions. We demand that they should be testable, that is, negatable. We discipline ourselves to entertain the negations. Science, we say, is self-corrective, by which we mean that we pursue the negations. Psychologically, as Freud has indicated, it is an aid in overcoming the repressions, of overcoming our wish for a tidy unnegated world and life. The entertainment of negation is a critical step in the scientific enterprise.

Let us now consider the "beyond," that is, the distinction between the manifest and the unmanifest, and the assertion of the reality of the unmanifest. The task of science is precisely to discover reality which is not immediately in evidence. The scientist has devised apparatus, microscopes, telescopes, clocks, and meters, which make manifest what is not manifest. Beyond this simple amplification of the senses his task is to find such regularities or principles in accordance with which phenomena take place. These, before his discovery of them, were hidden. His task is to make them manifest. It is much the same for the mystic. The mystic, Bertrand Russell (1953) tells us, has

> the conception of a Reality behind the world of appearance and utterly different from it. This Reality is regarded with an admiration often amounting to worship; it is felt to be always and everywhere close at hand, thinly veiled by the shows of sense, ready, for the receptive mind, to shine in its glory even through the apparent folly and wickedness of Man.

144

This could equally have been written to describe Newton and his laws of motion.

Consider psychoanalysis from this point of view. Freud is sometimes said to have "discovered" the unconscious. Actually the unconscious was under discussion before Freud. In the simple sense that "the unconscious" was something that no one knew existed, and then "discovered," Freud did not "discover" the unconscious. The significance of Freud's contribution was that he brought together in a meaningful way two major regions of the unmanifest. The first is the region of the unmanifest as it is ordinarily known in science, as the regularities in accordance with which phenomena operate. The second is that there is in the psyche of man much that is not present in awareness. Part of the significance of Freud's contribution was that it pointed out that there is a region of the psyche which is not manifest and which is important, and that there is a relationship between this region and the region of regularities that science had been concerned with. He brought together the unknown of science and the unknown of the human psyche. Between these two regions there are intimate connections. As a principal example, consider the Freudian discovery of "repression." Repression is that regularity, that is, an item in what was the unknown of science, whereby items become unknown in the psyche. Here we have a "law" concerning the unknown. It points up the way in which the two unknowns of science and psychoanalysis, to a degree to which the very unknown of each is already characterized, come together.

The relationship of psychoanalysis to mysticism in the approach to the unknown is extremely interesting. In primitive mysticism, the universe which is unknown is endowed with properties from the known. The *error* associated with the belief in the significance of the unmanifest is to endow the unmanifest with characteristics from the manifest. The contribution of psychoanalysis to this was to show the way in which this was a projection from the psyche, from features which were deep and unknown within it. The demonstration of this error of primitive mysticism is one of the outstanding characteristics of the psychoanalytic movement. Freud

145

took myth and showed that it was based on certain psychological characteristics.

A second step in Freud's thinking was to then take these psychological characteristics themselves and attempt to relate them to other universes such as the universe of human experience which exceeded the single individual, as in *Totem and Taboo* (1938) and the universe of the single-celled organism as in *Beyond the Pleasure Principle* (1950). As we are aware, most people are very selective in what they choose to take from Freud and what they choose not to take. And certainly the notions of primitive horde, the murder of the primeval father, and the death instinct, are among the notions which are the least palatable to the antimystical minds which seek to draw upon Freud's thought. I might say parenthetically that I believe that there is a process going on with respect to Freud such as went on with respect to Newton. As we know, Newton's more conspicuous mystical thought was suppressed by his rightist followers. I think the same thing has been going on with respect to Freud. The more conspicuously mystical parts of his thought are being suppressed or at least ignored by rightist psychoanalysts.

I think that this is a mistake. For I think that the more conspicuously mystical parts of Freud's thought are essential to our understanding of the total psychoanalytic enterprise; as, indeed, I think that our understanding of Newton would have been enhanced had the mystical part of his thinking not been suppressed. Certainly these writings are obscure. But when an author is writing of something which he cannot know whereof he speaks, except dimly, to use Wittgenstein's famous phrase, then he must write obscurely. If it is within the region of the unmanifest, then he can only write of it in an unclear way, the degree of clarity corresponding to the degree to which that of which he speaks is manifest.

The problem of the role of the senses in connection with knowledge is extremely interesting to us in terms of the distinction between the manifest and the unmanifest. In psychoanalytic practice every effort is made to reduce the stimulation of the senses. The room is darkened and made quiet. The patient lies down in such a way as to reduce the kinesthetic stimulation of his body. In every way the effort is made to reduce the sensory stimulation. It is precisely the informative senses with which we contact the world which interfere with the psychoanalytic efforts to contact the unmanifest. One of the important contributions of psychoanalytic theory is to have pointed out the significance of non-informative sensory stimulation in the psychological life of the individual, the stimulation of the surface of the body outside of the usual informative sense organs, the oral, anal, and genital regions of the body surface. According to Stace (1960) it is precisely those experiences which do not involve the informative sense organs which mark off the mystical experience. But an eminent scientist like Max Planck (1937) writes:

> Modern physics impresses us particularly with the old doctrine that there are realities existing apart from our sense-perceptions, and that there are problems and conflicts where these realities are of greater value for us than the richest treasures of the world of sense experience [p. 138].

Here is one of the important ways in which psychoanalysis, mysticism, and science come together: in the full awareness of the limitations associated with sticking too closely to data provided by the informative sense organs.

This brings us to our third major point: that it is possible and desirable to make portions of the unmanifest manifest by meditation. More generally, this is the belief that through engaging in certain specified intrapsychic processes it is possible to reach beyond the veil which covers the unmanifest; and that through the apprehension of what was unmanifest a radical overhaul of the human condition is possible.

In this respect we can consider mathematics, at least leftist mathematics, as perhaps one of the highest forms of meditation. That mathematics and mysticism both entail a deep commitment to meditation helps to explain why mathematics and mysticism have so often gone together. The relationship of logic (with mathematics

147

conceived as a branch of logic) to mysticism has been noted by Russell in the paper to which I referred earlier. In mathematics we seek to get at a kind of truth which is not manifest. We do it by means of a psychotechnical exercise. The reality to which we come is felt to be sounder than the ephemeral and unstable world of the informative sense organs. In mathematics there is that peculiar synthesis of discovery and invention which reaches out and comes to grips with the world in a way which would otherwise be completely impossible.

The possibility of radical reform of the condition of human existence through meditation is one of the central features of the mystical position. The mystic starts with the sense of alienation and ends with a sense of union with what was unmanifest. The mathematician ends up with the deep experience of relationship which he did not have before. In those forms of meditation which we call introspection, free association, dream interpretation, etc., we have the experience of insight, an experience based on the apprehension of what was not manifest before and with it the possibility of radical reform of the condition.

It is clear that the meditative exercise to the mystic, the discipline of logic, mathematics, and the scientific method, and of free association and dream interpretation can all be regarded as systematic forms of meditation, psychotechnical devices which are presumed to bring the individual into contact with regions of existence which would otherwise remain unmanifest. The objection that they differ from each other with respect to how much emotional or personal entailment there is in them does not really stand. For there are many mathematicians who "live for" their mathematics.

In each of the three modes of thought the ultimate appeal is to the experience of the individual. This is certainly the case in science, where, for example, so much stress has been made on such things as replicability, the fundamental idea being that a scientific truth is a truth which can be repeated for any individual if he but engages in the same procedures and "meditations." It is certainly the case in connection with mysticism which has always been related to a profound individualism as contrasted with authority and community. And it is certainly the case in psychoanalysis where the fundamental truths must be individually experienced in order to be understood and accepted. And somehow, at least in psychoanalysis and mysticism, this individual experience is the way to a radical modification in the life of the individual, especially in the modification of desire.

I will conclude by metaphorically and even obscurely elaborating on a hint from Freud's *Moses and Monotheism* (1955). In that essay Freud suggested that God was Aton, the sun. The sun throws light. It makes manifest what is otherwise unmanifest. To really understand one would have to make the very source of the manifest itself manifest; one would have to look at the sun. Yet if we looked into the sun we would become dazzled and blind. In order to look at the sun we must use some kind of a darkening device. If the darkening device is too opaque then we see nothing. If it is not opaque enough we are dazzled. I believe that this is the situation that we are in with respect to knowledge. Our darkening device is repression. When it is excessive we see very little indeed. But without repression we would be dazzled and blind and see nothing. The art which we need to cultivate is that of lifting the repression so that we can see as much as possible without being blinded by what we do behold.

♣ ♣ ♣ ♣ ♣ ♣ ♣ ♣ ♣ ♣ ♣ ♣ ♣ ♣ *14*

Idolatry in Religion and Science

"The keynote of idolatry is contentment with the present gods."—A. N. Whitehead.

There exists a view of the relationship between science and religion in which science is envisaged as preempting the role of religion. This view has it that in primitive times man needed answers to questions about his nature, creation, existence, and destiny, and that his need for answers was greater than his need for well-founded beliefs. His urgency made him create myths. These myths are the foundation of religion. In the enlightened present, this view continues, science has produced "better" answers to these questions.

The conclusions drawn from science have at times been sharply inconsistent with these religious myths.

Among those who share this view there have arisen a variety of strategies for coping with these inconsistencies. We can find the rejection of religion, the rejection of science, the "rationalization" of religion in the light of scientific enterprise itself, the attempt to draw sharp distinctions between the subject matter of religion and the subject matter of science, and so forth. I would like to sketch out yet another way of looking at the problem of the relationship between religion and science, using as a fulcrum the very ancient concept of idolatry. Idolatry, it would seem, is a terribly negative concept. I would hope, however, that the positive value of what may appear at first as a negative approach will soon emerge.

Although I am a psychologist it is not as a psychologist that I think of myself in the formulation of these ideas. I am fully aware that in the contemporary world psychology is one of the chief contenders for possession of domains religious, as well as the chief candidate for "Agent to Effect a Reconciliation Between Science and Religion." Psychology is a possible point of penetration between these two complexes of thought in that both, presumably, have something to do with the nature of man's mind, heart, or spirit, in one sense or another. I am afraid of psychological apologias for religion. I have more respect for the essential "truth" of religious insight and for the significance of the religious quest than to allow its admission to be dependent upon its coming in upon psychology's coattails. Allow me to divest myself of my psychologist's badge if it means that I am a scientific commando attacking religion, or even a medical aid man coming to patch up religion's wounds. Nor do I pretend to be a religionist. Although my interests in religion have been intense and long-lasting I would not in any way want to appear as an "expert" in religion. David Riesman commented once that the only people who were really qualified to be creative and objective about the contemporary world situation are the amateurs, because the experts have vested interests in the status quo and amateurs might possibly succeed where experts could not. Allow me then to take the posture of an amateur on the matter of the rela-

151

tionship of science and religion—and I sincerely hope that no one will challenge my amateur standing.

Perhaps you realize that I am advocating a kind of amateur standing for all in connection with the relationships between science and religion. A freshness of approach, such as I assume to be associated with amateur standing, is needed for coping with the issues; and the issues themselves arise out of a certain rigidity and a certain fixity in both religion and in science.

The fundamental impulse of both science and religion is the singular impulse of man to appreciate the nature of his existence in time, in space, in history, and in corporeality, and to appreciate the possibility of transcending any specific expression of his nature. All that falls under the heading of either science or religion issues from this singular impulse. The self-definition of man, in substance and in concept, is his most abiding characteristic beyond any specific definition; and both the scientific and the religious enterprises are expressions of this self-definitional activity. This impulse presupposes that the manifest is but the barest hint of reality, that beyond the manifest there exist the major portions of reality, and that the function of the impulse is to reach out toward the unmanifest.

From this singular and most restless impulse in man have come both science and religion; within science many little sciences; within religion many little religions; within science many scientific concepts; and within religion many religious concepts. This splintering of the expression of the impulse is necessary to the expression of the impulse, just as a long poem is the clarification of what is expressible in a single grunt.

The impulse moves toward the fulfillment of an objective; its essence is the motion toward and not the objective itself. In its impatience to realize fulfillment it may seek to satisfy itself more immediately. When man tarries too long, when man seeks to be completely fulfilled on the way towards the objective, when, in effect, he allows the impulse to be bribed, then he commits the sin of idolatry.

Sometimes I find myself perseverating over a word in connection with some problem long before I fully know exactly what

I am trying to tell myself. From the moment that I began thinking of the nature of this problem, the word "idolatry" has been rattling around among my thoughts. In the Talmud the question is raised as to the sins one may not commit even on pain of death. And the reply is given that there are three such sins—idolatry, adultery, and murder. Thus, in my thinking, idolatry is a very heinous kind of thing; and its very heinousness should make me pause, so as not to use the term wantonly. But then, I remind myself, I am a modern man! The prophets and the Talmud notwithstanding, idolatry, in the simple sense of the term, is much too silly a thing in the context of modernity to really worry about. If someone were to put a sword to my ribs to make me bow down before some graven image, I think I would do it readily, for such an act would be trivial for me, as trivial as the exercise of touching my toes without bending my knees. Yet I cannot say that the sin of idolatry is impossible for modern man to commit. For whatever was sinful in the idolatry of ancient times is still sinful. What is problematical is to determine exactly what idolatry could possibly mean to modern man. Thus I have misgivings over the use of a term which might possibly be outmoded and insignificant in the context of the modern world. And I have misgivings that if it is a significant thing in the context of modern times is it then not more than I want to take on? I am, as you see, uncertain of my clarity and weak in my conviction.

What I would say is that idolatry, a term I will presently attempt to define more relevantly, exists in both our scientific and religious enterprises; that idolatry is associated with their having been split apart as they have; and that idolatries of various kinds tend to maintain sharp inarticulation between them. What is so wrong about the worship of a graven image? Why did Jeremiah and Isaiah carry on so? Were they indeed simply taking the part of the God who was jealous of other gods? Was it simply, as it would seem, a kind of power struggle between gods? Or is there not something about the Judeo-Christian tradition which has some intrinsic features relevant to mankind—something to do with mankind not subjecting himself to abuse? Indeed I ask the question rhetorically. I use the term "idolatry" as I do because I think that

153

there exists a certain—even a certain fundamental—characteristic of the primitive forms of idolatry which has been repeated in both the science and religion of Western civilization. And, furthermore, the sickness of the spirit which is supposed to ensue from the practice of primitive idolatry is not too far removed from the sickness of the spirit toward which we address ourselves in the modern world.

As with primitive idolatry neither contemporary science nor contemporary religion is lacking in ardor. Idolatry is the worship of the means toward the fulfillment of the religious impulse as the fulfillment of the religious impulse. Put simply, engaging in ritual, painting religious pictures, reading religious literature, and such activities are not idolatrous unless they themselves become the *objects* of the worship, rather than the means towards the fulfillment of the religious impulse. Idolatry is the loss of the sense of search, of the sense of freshness of the experience. It is the overquick fixing upon any method or device or concept as the ultimate fulfillment of the religious impulse. Idolatry is allowing the impulse to be bribed by incomplete but immediate satisfaction. The use of religious objects as reminders, as sensory provocation, or the like, of the religious impulse is not idolatrous. What is idolatrous is the frame of mind that allows them to be ultimate.

What I am saying is of course not novel to the Judeo-Christian tradition and especially not to the ethical part of this tradition. Running throughout the Judeo-Christian tradition is the message that one should not settle for easy and immediate satisfaction of the impulse life, that the satisfaction of an impulse should be appropriate to the impulse, and that the religious impulse should have its satisfaction in God. The worship of one's self, the sin of pride, is idolatrous in that it is an impulse which should be directed toward God. The sexual impulse should not be spent except upon the proper object. The aggressive impulse should be spent only upon him who is truly an enemy. Jeremiah, the fearful warner against backsliding, helps us to understand the significance of idolatry. Idolatry, he says, makes the people "provoke themselves to the confusion of their own faces" (Jeremiah 7:19). We could grow so-

154

phisticated and talk about the way in which the pluralism, and the tendency to fix upon each item in the contemporary plural, have produced a problem in identity, but Jeremiah's "provoke themselves to the confusion of their own faces" catches at the problem effectively.

I yield to the temptation of identifying idolatry as I have defined it with the picture of contemporary neurosis. I believe that there is probably a relationship between psychological difficulty and sin as has been suggested by Professor Mowrer, if not exactly in the sense that he has suggested. The thing about the sin of idolatry, at least in the way in which I understand it, is that it is so costly to the person. I am not sure that I can specify exactly the nature of psychological cost for one or another enterprise that the human being engages in, but there is little question that the psychological cost is great. It is a most expensive kind of indulgence. The neurosis is a kind of fixity or rigidity at a certain stage of development. It is to become arrested at a way station and usually for the small satisfaction that is to be had at that stage. In the neurosis the individual continues to struggle to win a kind of satisfaction from the old when in fact he should be working toward the future for its greater, fresher gratification. As Fenichel (1945) puts it, the essential feature of neurotic behavior is that "patients, instead of reacting vividly to actual stimuli, according to their specific nature, react repeatedly with rigid patterns." My definition of idolatry conceives of it as a kind of "being stuck" in the pursuit of the fulfillment of the basic religious impulse. The neurosis too is a matter of being stuck at a particular way of fulfilling the impulses of the person.

Consider for the moment this God of the Judeo-Christian tradition, this God who asserted his identity and forbade idolatry. I am no theologian and would not want to enter into any pursuit of the nature of God. But as a religious conception I would regard this as an act of religious genius (and I submit that I have difficulty in fully understanding the distinction between conception and revelation). This God was a God made single, invisible, ubiquitous, and I think, most importantly, a God with whom contact was always a bit dubious. The very dubiousness of grace in the thought of Calvin is, I think, one of the great features of his thought. This was indeed a concept of God which could serve the religious impulse of mankind in a way which would not do violence to man's nature. Never could mankind have the sense of closure in contact with this God and yet the contact with this God was always in the realm of possibility, even if it be unknown whether at any time, or for any individual, such contact could be. This is the paradoxical feature of this God, that of possible yet dubious contact, contact always possibly available, and yet in doubt—a God, and I think that this is critical, knowable in the limited region of the expression of his nature (in a piece of the world, a concretization in parts of man, and so forth) but not ultimately knowable. This was a God to be continuously worked toward, a God who was as continuous, as frustrating, and as fulfilling as life itself. The commandment against idolatry was a commandment to believe that complete substantial contact with God could never take place. The substantial contact with God must always be in the nature of a search. One must always be filled with a sense of wonder of what was not yet reached. One must always be yearning toward fulfillment, but fulfillment must be maintained as an ideal. Fulfillment was always away, and seeming fulfillment always mythical, at least, and, more than likely, idolatrous. The genius of the concept of God so developed inheres in the very fact that a certain lack of completion was always involved. For in this lack of completion is contained the means whereby man can maintain the freshness of experience that experience demands.

The God of Western man is conceived of as playing a grand and cosmic game of peekaboo with mankind. Perhaps only in this game is God relevant to man. He insists that he shall play peekaboo with man. Freud once pointed out that the satisfaction of games like peekaboo for a child consists in learning to control an environment of which he feels fearful, and with respect to which he wishes to achieve some mastery. Through the playing of peekaboo a child trains himself for the time when his parents do leave him. In the game it is a playful leaving and, by virtue of its play character, it is less threatening. So perhaps it is with mankind at large. Mankind has developed a concept of God with whom he forever plays peek-aboo, and through it manages to learn how to manage his life. When the day comes that he clings to an image of the ever-present God as the real one, and therefore, in effect, stops the game of peekaboo with God, then he loses out on the fundamental value of the game.

The history of the Judeo-Christian religion is filled with instances in which a means of fulfilling the religious impulse became the object of worship itself; and the history is also filled with instances in which people became discontented with such idolatrous tendencies and reaffirmed the fundamental religious quest with the rejection of the idolatrous objects, substituting a renewed search for the seeming satisfaction.

Let us now consider science. The scientific impulse and the religious impulse are not nearly as separate as some modern thought might lead one to believe. To point to the religiosity of people like Newton, Kepler, Fechner, and others cannot be taken as a priori evidence for the view that the impulses are the same. But the dynamics of the relationship become a bit clearer in a figure like that of Jonathan Edwards, the Puritan minister. To study the nature of God was his obligation. The God whom he had in his thoughts was a God of a self-distancing nature, who predestined the universe. How did this predestination of God work itself out? For Jonathan Edwards, Newton almost literally opened up the sky. God had predestined the world by fashioning the world-machine as Newton had conceived it. He had given it a shove and had made the law of inertia, and then the universe carried on and would thus carry on unto eternity. To study the physics of Newton was then to study the nature of God. In Edwards' thought God's omnipresence is translated into the equation of God and space. In the mind of a man like Edwards the acceptance of Newtonian mechanics, later to become the chief competitor of the religious outlook, is the answer to the problem of how to know God. It is the means for the knowledge of God.

The mechanical conception of the nature of the universe has for several centuries been one of the major pawns in the struggle between religion and science. It has sometimes been offered as a major contender for a concept of the nature of the universe to replace what presumably is held by the exponents of the Judeo-Christian tradition. In the minds of many intellectuals who have grown up in the last century the question has seemed to be that of making a choice between the one and the other because of seeming incompatibility between them.

It is my opinion that the degree of strain between religion and science is the direct function of the degree of idolatry, as I have defined it, in both religion and science. The Bible is indeed one of the finest expressions and means of fulfillment of the religious impulse. Yet to make it the end of worship and devotion is idolatrous. It is only when the Bible is idolatrously worshipped that it can be seriously threatened by either the Darwinian theory of evolution, the discovery of the Law of Moses in Hammurabi, or the "higher criticism" of the Bible which gives it a later date than is commonly believed and an origin less than that of divine revelation in the simple sense.

Similarly the mechanical conception of the nature of the universe was a magnificent intellectual achievement in the way of coming to an understanding of the operation of the heavenly bodies and matter in motion on the earth itself. Yet especially in the nineteenth century the mechanical conception of the nature of the universe became the object of idolatrous worship. It became in time not something to consider or even to believe in, but an item of faith such that the challenge of it was considered unscientific (a word which was used almost synonymously with blasphemous). In some scientific circles, to challenge the proposition that the universe was exhaustively explainable in terms of matter and motion could only be labelled as "heretical." Yet I would maintain that this worship of the mechanical conception was as idolatrous as any religious activity could be.

Insofar as the scientific enterprise is concerned, the disease of idolatry has been dubbed the disease of methodolatry, the worship of method. In terms of our conception of idolatry it is certainly the case that certain ways have been of value and will continue to be of value in exploring the nature of man and the world and their relationships. However, when there is a worship of these methods themselves rather than the objective toward which they are directed, then indeed does science become idolatrous.

As I have indicated, in both science and religion there is the assumption that the fundamental reality is what is beyond the manifest. And no matter how far our explorations go, and no matter how much we manage to uncover, there is always the huge world of the unmanifest. If at any stage of development we begin to worship the manifest or the means whereby we have made some part manifest, then indeed can it be said that we are being idolatrous.

If it were possible to root our idolatrous tendencies in both science and religion, then the singularity of the impulse expressed in both science and religion would emerge with clarity. It is not that religion, as some have maintained, supplies mythical answers until science can provide more valid ones. Rather it is that both religion and science are attempts on the part of mankind to search out the nature of himself and the world in which he lives. But it is search rather than answer which is significant. Indeed, as soon as either the scientist or the theologian allows himself to be fixed upon an answer as though it were the ultimate fulfillment of his impulse, then indeed does he stop being either scientist or theologian and becomes an idolater.

Psychological Characteristics of Man Projected in the Image of Satan

Adolf Eichmann was a man who had been the director of the most enormous holocaust in the history of the world. He had been captured. A trial was held with him literally under glass, open to inspection for the world. In the contemporary world social scientists neither want to be, nor are able to be, isolated from the world of real events; and it is somehow desirable for them to study social events *in vivo*. Eichmann challenges the scientific role. Enough had been heard about so called "scientific experiments" conducted under the Nazis. On hearing of these "scientific experiments" one might rather not be a scientist. I once heard a colleague say that the "trouble with those experiments was that they were so badly done from a scientific point of view." One becomes pensive. Suppose that they had been done impeccably from a scientific point of view. Would that have justified them? The presentation of the matter of Eichmann and the enormity of the Nazi holocaust is a kind of extreme challenge to the "non-violence" that is sometimes atmospherically associated with a value-suspending social science.

One of the major problems associated with the attempt to comprehend evil is that our morality itself, our aversion to evil, makes us tend to be aversive to looking at evil long enough to get to understand it. I would think that it is very important to recognize that thinking of evil is not evil. One of the important lessons which has been taught to us with the advent of the psychoanalytic movement has been that it is in repression that there is the worst evil. There is a sense in which it is the case that evil inheres in the tendency not to look at evil; and the overcoming of evil inheres in the courage to look at it.

I will allow myself what appears to be a beginning violation of "non-violence" by saying that Eichmann brings to mind the figure of Satan. There are some dramatic similarities. One may speculate that the designers of the concentration camps had been strongly influenced by the classical images of what Hell was supposed to be like. Eichmann was the archdevil, master of hells which bore names like Auschwitz and Bergen-Belsen, the "angel of death" for millions. There were death and pain and fires and ingenious mechanical contrivances of torment. And, importantly, those who were instrumental in their creation and management had some sense of being under some grand cosmic directive. When they captured Eichmann, he turned out to be a very ungrandiose type of person, a bureaucrat who, as he said of himself, sat at his desk and did his job. It is exactly this copresence of both the banal and the grandiose which is a major hint concerning the nature of evil.

There are some very close links between what I will call an ultrarealism and an ultramythicism on the one hand, and evil on

161

the other. Both ultrarealism and ultramythicism were entailed in the Nazi holocaust, and both are entailed in the historical image of Satan. I believe that the consideration of this image might then help us to understand something concerning the nature of evil.

One might well ask what a self-respecting contemporary psychologist with even some scientific pretensions may be doing considering so mythical a thing as the image of Satan. My purpose is to take advantage of the centuries of human symbol formation in which the image of Satan emerged as the representative and the personification of evil. I would thus hope that by the consideration of this image our understanding of the nature of evil might be increased. One of the most valuable ways of apprehending the nature of the human mind is through the images that it creates. In modern times we have an aversion to fantasy for fear that it might distort our perception of reality. But this should not interfere with our investigation of fantasy in order to apprehend the nature of personality which engages in fantasy. I am following the pattern which was set some years ago when Henry A. Murray read a paper (Murray, 1962) on the psychological meanings of Satan. In that presentation Murray defended his enterprise with some words that I should like to repeat:

> The ground for this undertaking of mine, as well as for the hope that other psychologists will invade the abundant field of religious "imagents" and images, and grapple with one or another of its many mysteries, is a conclusion, or value judgment, I have come to, on the periphery of science, which might be termed a credo. It is the belief that the evidence set forth by anthropologists and psychoanalysts, particularly by Frazer and by Freud, in favor of the proposition that religions are products of human imaginations revised by rationality, is so massive and persuasive that it adds up to a veritable discovery, potentially the most consequential since Darwin's theory of evolution.

I should like to point out that my interpretation of the image of Satan is different, but not inconsistent with, Murray's. But fantasy is itself inexhaustive of its meanings, and the image of Satan is particularly heavily invested with meaning.

The image of Satan is both ultrarealistic and ultramythic. The ultrarealism is manifest, in the first place, by the inordinate sense of his reality, in spite of his mythic quality, by those in the history of Western civilization who have claimed to have known him. There is little question of his complete phenomenological reality in the encounter that Jesus had with him or in most of the history of Western civilization. Indeed, Satan is, for those who believe in him, the embodiment of the real. When he is presumed to be at work he is real, and all other things, which are commonly taken as the real, are the illusions that he creates. Satan's reality is certainly greater than the reality presented by the senses. Historically this has been one of the charges made against persons who have played roles in the history of science: that the evidence of their senses was "really" the delusions placed by Satan. And the inquisitors had little doubt about the reality of Satan, all of the evidence to the contrary to which they were witness notwithstanding. Indeed, they took evidence against what they believed as proof of his existence, that very evidence attesting to his power. The logic may have been poor, but logic is no match for clear phenomenological reality as was the case in connection with Satan. It is this attribution of great "reality" to some limited part of the phenomenological field that I refer to as ultrarealism.

What is thus concretised in the image of Satan is the more general characteristic of ultrarealism. The ultrarealism is also manifested in the making of a very firm distinction between what is "me" and what is "not-me." In the case of Satan this is manifested in the fact that Satan is most often experienced as "out there" and alien to the ego. Our contemporary psychological wisdom has made us profoundly aware of how it can be that something which is experienced intensely as alien to the ego is still very much the product of the psyche which created it. Satan as alien to the ego was experienced as "really" alien to the ego. One might go so far as to suggest that Satan is the paradigmatic projection. In, say, the

Thematic Apperception Test or the Rorschach there is a varying degree of phenomenological "out-thereness" associated with the responses, which may be taken as the degree of "projection" involved in the responses. In the case of Satan, this phenomenological "out-thereness" is characteristically very extreme.

The image of Satan is characteristically associated with pains and with pleasures. Pains and pleasures are characteristically associated with the action of externals on the body. And these pains and pleasures are intimately tied up with the placing of the necessity for human action on things which are external to the psyche. This brings us to what I consider to be one of the most important features for the understanding of the nature of evil. The ultrarealism of Satan is associated with an intense externalization of internal necessity. In the myth of Satan this is often expressed in the notion of Satan as the tempter, the external manipulator of pains and pleasures whereby the individual is forced to act in one way or another in recognition of the imperative associated with the external power to create pain and pleasure. The ultrarealism consists in the projection of "reality" on the external sources of pain and pleasure. People who have been "possessed" have engaged in various types of actions under what seems to be external compulsion. Freud (1950), in his paper on demoniacal possession, identified this condition with the condition of the neurotic. One of the characteristics of the neurotic is exactly this: that his behavior appears to be determined by external forces, when in point of fact we know that the force for the action arises from internal sources. Thus the identification of possession with neurosis is not so far fetched. This conversion of internal necessity so that it appears as external necessity, so clear in the image of Satan, is one of the essential features of evil, whether there is a literal imagery of Satan or not.

Let us go back to Eichmann. Eichmann's defense was that he acted under external rather than internal demands, and that by virtue of his position as a "cog" he was subject without choice to these external necessities. The prosecution essentially attempted to demonstrate that he acted on the basis of internal necessity. And this was the issue in the trial. I am not interested in rerunning the trial of Eichmann. Rather, I would like to point out that, in the same way that external necessity is associated with the figure of Satan, so it is in the case of Eichmann's defense. The externalization of internal necessity is a precondition for engaging in evil, and ultrarealism is one form of such externalization. It is often the case that persons who engage in evil believe that they do so in cognizance and in response to the demands of external necessity. It is often the case that "in the name of the real" is the façade for "in nomine diaboli." However, close examinattion of the "real" will often demonstrate that its high degree of phenomenological "reality" is itself illusory, as is characteristic of projection generally. The deliberate infliction of pain and death on others often has associated with it an "I was forced to do it" by an illusory externalized necessity.

There are other manifestations of this ultrarealism which are closely related to evil. Response to the manifestations of pain in others is repressed. There is cynicism, repression of affect and sympathy, repression of perception and thought. In the name of "reality" interpersonal relations are guided by formal contractual relations and the assessment of the sources of pains and pleasures exclusively.

One other important association of the image of Satan is with the world of material things. Not too long ago science, especially that form of science which sought to define all of nature in terms of matter and motion and concerned itself with pulleys and gears and screws, was identified with Satan. I do not mean to suggest that we go back to that position. However, it might be worth our while to have a look at what meaning the change may possibly have had. In modern times we have grown accustomed to think of engineering largely in the service of peace and bounty. One of the characteristics of Satan throughout history is that he has been extremely able in coping with the material world and a master of ingenious and artful physical and chemical devices. Historically, however, such engineering skill was more largely associated with death and with pain in the form of instruments of warfare and of torture. The historical images of Hell have been filled with "clever" torture devices. Throughout history the screw was used as a torture device more often than as part of machines that had other purposes than infliction of pain. The artfulness of the gas chambers and the ovens and the "scientific" experiments of Eichmann may be understood as a regression to an earlier form of "realism."

Murray suggested that the Satanic spirit prevailed within the field of psychology especially among those who were most self-consciously scientific in a certain manner. I cannot resist pointing out that within the field of psychology there exist several forms which can readily be identified with what I have been calling ultra-realism. I do not mean to suggest that we revert to some condition preceding the scientific age. I would only indicate that the conception of living organisms in the limited "realism" of matter is such that death and life are indistinguishable, and the pain of another person has no "reality."

The ultrarealistic is often combined with an ultramythic. On the face of it it would appear that the ultrarealistic and the ultramythic are so disparate that they cannot coexist. Psychologists, however, are well aware of how deeply incompatible modes exist side by side within the same person, often reinforcing each other, often raising both to heights in the reaction of the one to the other. Both prevailed together among the Nazis. I am inclined to believe that the combination of the two is extremely important in most of the organized and widespreading evils of the history of the world.

By ultramythicism I mean the preoccupation with a mythical world and believing that the events of one's life are the playing out of some grand cosmic drama. It was undoubtedly with a sense of such a role in a grand cosmic drama that the decision was made for the "final solution of the Jewish question." It is unnecessary to go into the details of this cosmic drama as it was spelled out by Adolf Hitler. I would only point out that when the Nazis persecuted the Jews they were not psychologically interacting with those individuals but rather with fantasized, fictional beings in the drama in which they felt themselves to be a part. It was a drama which reached far into history and into imaginative spaces far beyond the limited lives of the participants.

In the image of Satan we also have that ultramythic quality, which is, of course, one of the most prominent characteristics of the image. The universe in which Satan lives is the same universe as that of God and the angels. Indeed, he has had a presumptive history of being rather close to God in the first place before his "fall." He is, on the one hand, more grandiose than any human being could ever be, and, on the other hand, he is willing to consort with human beings. But he does constitute a kind of contact with that "other" universe.

It was this ultramythic quality which we associate with evil that made the actual appearance of Eichmann something of a shock. Our image of the designers of evil, conditioned by, say, Milton's *Paradise Lost,* in which Satan is depicted as being of some momentous stature, contrasted sharply with the undistinguished little bureaucrat. He was hardly a person to be master of the grandest Hell that had ever been fashioned in the concrete.

The ultramythic feature of Satan appears to be quite inconsistent with the ultrarealistic, and yet they are present simultaneously. What is it then that makes it possible for the two sets of characteristics to be combined? It is that characteristic which we identified in ultrarealism, namely, the externalization of necessity which is common to both the ultrarealistic and the ultramythic, both of which get combined in the image of Satan. In both instances one acts in accordance with what appear to be external demands, whether they be the demands of "reality" or the demands of the cosmic. The ultramythic is very important in that it places the burden of the act upon the cosmic, in contrast to the noncosmic being that the person himself is.

What we need to understand is that the banal is the denial of the cosmic, which is itself at the basis of the evil. The contradiction between the ultrarealistic and the ultramythic is a way of preserving what is common to both, the externalization of necessity. If one were to charge Eichmann or any other person who has engaged in evil by pointing out the defects of the cosmic, he would argue that he is really realistic. If one were to charge the inquisitor with realism, he would argue that he is involved in something cosmic. But in going from one to the other, the issue of the externalization of necessity remains untouched. It is actually no accident at all that the greatest of evils in the history of the world have been engaged in by people who felt that they "had no choice." For, most of the time, evil is helped out by a variety of psychological processes which tend to give phenomenological external demand character, and thus one has no choice but to respond to such inexorable appearing demands. It has sometimes been commented that one of the outstanding characteristics of the Devil is that he does not appear to be the Devil. We can translate this into more secular terms. The profoundest psychological feature associated with the image of Satan is projection. In particular the use of projection is to externalize demand upon the individual. But acting on the basis of external demand rather than internal demand does not appear as evil; it only works out that way.

Let me try to pull some of this together somewhat more closely. The problem of evil is at question, and the Nazi holocaust is the outstanding example. One stands witness in the present century to the use of the products of science and engineering and social organization for the infliction of death and pain, and asks for meanings. When men were less effective generally they were less capable of inflicting death and pain. When they became more capable they used that capability for inflicting more death and pain, so that by any measure the Nazi holocaust was the most enormous. We take two hints, one from psychology—that religious images are about man—and one from religion—that Satan is representative of evil. We find that within the image of Satan there appear to be at least two complexes, ultrarealism combined with ultramythicism, and that this has hardly ever been looked upon as a defect of the Satan image. Considering both ultrarealism and ultramythicism, however, seems to indicate that there is a common factor; this common factor seems to be the externalization of necessity, that is, in both the ultrarealistic and the ultramythic, the determination of

168

behavior is based on factors which appear to the individual as external to the individual.

We seem to be at the door of the problem of freedom versus determinism and the classical tired considerations in connection with this issue tend to rush in. But perhaps there is an alternative way of dealing with this question, a way which can be informed by what Murray regarded as the most consequential discovery of modern times, that man projects his own characteristics.

Suppose that in one way or another we were to teach this discovery to the world at large, and especially the relationship of this mechanism to evil in the world. Somebody once said that the Puritan knew good from bad by internal cues. If it felt bad it was good; and if it felt good it was bad. We need to go beyond this. We need to learn that when one experiences a strong sense of external demand to cause pain or death this may be illusory, and only the projection of internal demand. Suppose we would also teach— and of course I mean this in the largest sense of the word—that there seem to be at least two ways of giving substance to this kind of projection, one being an ultrarealism and the other being an ultramythicism. Suppose we teach the essential invalidity of an ultrarealism, in the same way that we generally teach the essential invalidity of an ultramythicism. In a world in which there is such possibility of inflicting death and pain, our only hope is in the proper education of human beings, of enhancing their understanding, and especially of that tendency of the human psyche to make his internal demands appear to himself as external demands. The ultimate solution can come only by insight and understanding of the psychodynamic mechanism, which we are coming to appreciate as the essence of healing.

Bibliography

ACH, N. *Über die Willenstätigkeit und das Denken.* Göttingen: Vandenhoeck und Ruprecht, 1905.

BAILYN, B. *Education in the Forming of American Society.* Chapel Hill: University of North Carolina Press, 1960.

BAKAN, D. *Sigmund Freud and the Jewish Mystical Tradition.* Princeton: Van Nostrand, 1958.

BARNARD, G. A. Sampling Inspection and Statistical Decisions. *Journal of the Royal Statistical Society* (B), 1954, *16*, 151–165.

171

BERGMANN, G., and SPENCE, K. W. Operationism and Theory in Psychology. *Psychological Review*, 1941, *48*, 1–14.

BERGMANN, G., and SPENCE, K. W. The Logic of Psychophysical Measurement. *Psychological Review*, 1944, *51*, 1–24.

BERKSON, J. Some Difficulties of Interpretation Encountered in the Application of the Chi-square Test. *Journal of the American Statistical Association*, 1938, *33*, 526–542.

BERKSON, J. Tests of Significance Considered as Evidence. *Journal of the American Statistical Association*, 1942, *37*, 325–335.

BERLYNE, D. E. Attention, Perception and Behavior Theory. *Psychological Review*, 1951, *58*, 137–146.

BERNSTEIN, A. L. Temporal Factors in the Formation of Conditioned Eyelid Reactions in Human Subjects. *Journal of General Psychology*, 1934, *10*, 173–197.

BINDER, A. Further Considerations on Testing the Null Hypothesis and the Strategy and Tactics of Investigating Theoretical Models. *Psychological Review*, 1963, *70*, 101–109.

BOLLES, R. C. The Difference Between Statistical Hypotheses and Scientific Hypotheses. *Psychological Reports*, 1962, *11*, 639–645.

BOOLE, G. *The Laws of Thought*. Chicago: Open Court, 1940.

BORING, E. G. The Stimulus-Error. *American Journal of Psychology*, 1921, *32*, 449–471.

BORING, E. G. *A History of Experimental Psychology*. (2nd Ed.) New York: Appleton-Century-Crofts, 1950.

BORING, E. G. A History of Introspection. *Psychological Bulletin*, 1953, *50*, 169–189.

BRENTANO, F. *Psychologie vom empirischen Standpunkte*. Leipzig: Duncker und Humblot, 1874.

BRIDGMAN, P. W. *The Logic of Modern Physics*. New York: Macmillan, 1938.

BROWN, N. O. *Life Against Death: The Psychoanalytical Meaning of History*. Middletown, Conn.: Wesleyan University Press, 1959.

BÜHLER, K. Tatsachen und Probleme zu einer Psychologie der Denkvorgänge: I. Ueber Gedanken. *Archiv für gesamte Psychologie*, 1907, *9*, 297–365.

BURTT, E. A. *The Metaphysical Foundations of Modern Physical Science*. New York: Doubleday, 1954.

BUTTERFIELD, H. *The Statecraft of Machiavelli*. London: B. G. Bell, 1940.

CAMPBELL, A. A. The Interrelations of Two Measures of Conditioning in Man. *Journal of Experimental Psychology*, 1938, *22*, 225–243.

CARGILL, O. *Intellectual America: Ideas on the March.* New York: Macmillan, 1941.

COHEN, J. The Statistical Power of Abnormal-Social Psychological Research: A Review. *Journal of Abnormal and Social Psychology*, 1962, *65*, 145–153.

CRONBACH, L. J. The Two Disciplines of Scientific Psychology. *American Psychologist*, 1957, *12*, 671–684.

DE MORGAN, A. *An Essay on Probabilities.* London: Longman, 1849.

DEWEY, J. The Reflex Arc Concept in Psychology. *Psychological Review*, 1896, *3*, 357–370.

DEWEY, J. *Reconstruction in Philosophy.* New York: Mentor Books, 1950.

DURKHEIM, E. *Suicide: A Study in Sociology.* Glencoe, Ill.: The Free Press, 1951.

EDWARDS, A. L. *Experimental Design in Psychological Research.* New York: Rinehart, 1950.

EDWARDS, W., LINDMAN, H., and SAVAGE, L. J. Bayesian Statistical Inference for Psychological Research. *Psychological Review*, 1963, *70*, 193–242.

ERIKSON, E. H. *Childhood and Society.* (2nd Ed.) New York: Norton, 1963.

FENICHEL, O. *The Psychoanalytic Theory of Neurosis.* New York: Norton, 1945.

FERGUSON, L. *Statistical Analysis in Psychology and Education.* New York: McGraw-Hill, 1959.

FISHER, R. A. Statistical Methods and Scientific Induction. *Journal of the Royal Statistical Society* (B), 1955, *17*, 69–78.

FISHER, R. A. *The Design of Experiments.* (4th Ed.) Edinburgh: Oliver & Boyd, 1947.

FREUD, S. *Beyond the Pleasure Principle.* Translated by J. Strachey. New York: Liveright, 1950.

FREUD, S. *Moses and Monotheism.* New York: Vintage, 1955.

FREUD, S. A Neurosis of Demoniacal Possession in the Seventeenth Century. In *Collected Papers,* Volume IV. London: Hogarth, 1950.

FREUD, S. Negation. In *Collected Papers,* Volume V. London: Hogarth, 1952.

FREUD, S. Psychoanalysis: Freudian School. *Encyclopedica Britannica,* 14th Ed., 1929, vol. 18, pp. 672–674.

FREUD, S. *The Interpretation of Dreams.* In *Basic Writings.* New York: Modern Library, 1938.

GUILFORD, J. P. *Psychometric Methods.* New York: McGraw-Hill, 1936.

HARLOW, H. F. The Formation of Learning Sets. *Psychological Review,* 1949, *56,* 51–65.

HATHAWAY, S. R., and MCKINLEY, J. *Minnesota Multiphasic Personality Inventory Manual.* New York: Psychological Corp., 1951.

HEBB, D. O. Temperament in Chimpanzees. I. Methods of Analysis. *Journal of Comparative Physiological Psychology,* 1949, *42,* 192–206.

HERBART, J. F. *Joh. Fr. Herbart's Sämtliche Werke.* (Ed. K. Kehrbach.) Langensalza: H. Beyer und Söhne, 1887–1912.

HILGARD, E. R. *Theories of Learning.* New York: Appleton-Century, 1948.

HILGARD, E. R., and MARQUIS, D. G. *Conditioning and Learning.* New York: Appleton-Century, 1940.

HILGARD, J. R. Anniversary Reaction in Parents Precipitated by Children. *Psychiatry,* 1953, *16,* 73–80.

HODGES, J. L., and LEHMAN, E. L. Testing the Approximate Validity of Statistical Hypotheses. *Journal of the Royal Statistical Society* (B), 1954, *16,* 261–268.

HULL, C. L. *Principles of Behavior.* New York: Appleton-Century, 1943.

HULL, C. L., HOVLAND, C. I., ROSS, R. T., HALL, M., PERKINS, D. T., and FITCH, F. B. *Mathematico-Deductive Theory of Rote Learning.* New Haven: Yale University Press, 1940.

HUME, D. *A Treatise of Human Nature.* (Ed. L. A. Selby-Bigge.) Oxford: Clarendon Press, 1951.

HUNTER, W. S. Conditioning and Extinction in the Rat. *British Journal of Psychology,* 1935, *26,* 135–148.

JEFFRIES, H. *Scientific Inference.* New York: Macmillan, 1931.

KAISER, H. F. Directional Statistical Decision. *Psychological Review,* 1960, *67,* 160–167.

KATONA, G. *Organizing and Memorizing.* New York: Columbia University Press, 1940.

KEYNES, J. M. *A Treatise on Probability*. London: Macmillan, 1948.

KRIS, E. *Psychoanalytic Explorations in Art*. New York: International Universities Press, 1952.

LACEY, O. L. *Statistical Methods in Experimentation*. New York: Macmillan, 1953.

LINDQUIST, E. F. *Statistical Analysis in Educational Research*. Boston: Houghton Mifflin, 1940.

MATEER, R. *Child Behavior*. Boston: Badger, 1918.

MAYER, A., and ORTH, J. Zur qualitätiven Untersuchung der Association. *Zeitschrift der Psychologische und Physiologische Sinnesorganen*, 1901, *26*, 1–13.

MCCLELLAND, D. C. *The Achieving Society*. Princeton: Van Nostrand, 1961.

MCDOUGALL, W. Prolegomena to Psychology. *Psychological Review*, 1922, *29*, 1–43.

MCNEMAR, Q. At Random: Sense and Nonsense. *American Psychologist*, 1960, *15*, 295–300.

MELTON, A. W. Editorial. *Journal of Experimental Psychology*, 1962, *64*, 553–557.

MERLAN, P. Brentano and Freud. *Journal of the History of Ideas*, 1945, *6*, 375–377.

MERLAN, P. Brentano and Freud—a sequel. *Journal of the History of Ideas*, 1949, *10*, 451.

MERTON, R. K. Puritanism, Pietism, and Science. *Sociological Review*, 1936, *28*, 1–30.

MESSER, A. Experimentell-psychologische Untersuchung über das Denken. *Archiv für gesamte Psychologie*, 1906, *8*, 1–224.

MEYER, M. *The Psychology of the Other One*. Columbia, Missouri: Missouri Book Co., 1921.

MILL, J. S. *On Liberty*. New York: Appleton-Century-Crofts, 1947.

MUNRO, R. Anthropology. In J. Hastings (Ed.), *Encyclopedia of Religion and Ethics*. New York: Scribner, 1909.

MURRAY, H. A. The Personality and Career of Satan. *Journal of Social Issues*, 1962, *18*, 36–54.

NAGEL, E. Principles of the Theory of Probability. *International Encyclopedia of Unified Science*, 1, No. 6. Chicago: University of Chicago Press, 1947.

NEYMAN, J. Outline of a Theory of Statistical Estimation Based on the Classical Theory of Probability. *Philosophical Transactions of the Royal Society* (A), 1937, *236,* 333–380.

NEYMAN, J. "Inductive Behavior" as a Basic Concept of Philosophy of Science. *Review of the Mathematical Statistics Institute,* 1957, *25,* 7–22.

NEYMAN, J., and PEARSON, E. S. On the Problem of the Most Efficient Tests of Statistical Hypotheses. *Philosophical Transactions of the Royal Society* (A), 1933, *231,* 289–337.

NUNNALLY, J. The Place of Statistics in Psychology. *Education and Psychological Measurement,* 1960, *20,* 641–650.

PEARSON, E. S. Statistical Concepts in Their Relation to Reality. *Journal of the Royal Statistical Society* (B), 1955, *17,* 204–207.

PIAGET, J. *Logic and Psychology.* Manchester: Manchester University Press, 1953.

PLANCK, M. *The Universe in the Light of Modern Physics.* (Translated by W. H. Johnston.) London: Allen & Unwin, 1937.

REDLICH, F. C., and HOLLINGSHEAD, A. B. *Social Class and Mental Illness.* New York: Wiley, 1958.

REIK, T. *Listening with the Third Ear.* New York: Farrar & Strauss, 1948.

ROBERTS, C. L., and WIST, E. An Empirical Sidelight on the Aggregate-General Distinction. (Unpublished manuscript.)

ROGERS, C. R. *On Becoming a Person.* Boston: Houghton Mifflin, 1961.

ROSENTHAL, R., and GAITO, J. The Interpretation of Levels of Significance by Psychological Researchers. *Journal of Psychology,* 1963, *55,* 33–38.

ROZEBOOM, W. W. The Fallacy of the Null-Hypothesis Significance Test. *Psychological Bulletin,* 1960, *57,* 416–428.

RUSSELL, B. *Mysticism and Logic and Other Essays.* London: Penguin Books, 1953.

SAVAGE, L. J. *The Foundations of Statistics.* New York: Wiley, 1954.

SCHLAIFFER, R. *Probability and Statistics for Business Decisions.* New York: McGraw-Hill, 1959.

SHANNON, C. E., and WEAVER, W. *The Mathematical Theory of Communication.* Urbana: University of Illinois Press, 1949.

SHOCK, N. W. Growth Curves. In S. S. Stevens (Ed.), *Handbook of Experimental Psychology.* New York: Wiley, 1951.

SIDMAN, M. A Note on Functional Relations Obtained from Group Data. *Psychological Bulletin,* 1952, *49,* 263–269.

SKAGGS, E. B. The Limitations of Scientific Psychology as an Applied or Practical Science. *Psychological Review,* 1934, *41,* 572–576.

SKINNER, B. F. Are Theories of Learning Necessary? *Psychological Review,* 1950, *57,* 193–216.

SMITH, C. A. B. Review of N. T. J. Bailey, *Statistical Methods in Biology. Applied Statistics,* 1960, *9,* 64–66.

SNEDECOR, G. W. *Statistical Methods.* (4th Ed.) Ames: Iowa State College Press, 1946.

SOROKIN, P. *Altruistic Love.* Boston: Beacon Press, 1950.

SPENCE, K. W. The Nature of Theory Construction in Contemporary Psychology. *Psychological Review,* 1944, *51,* 47–68.

STACE, W. T. *The Teachings of the Mystics.* New York: Mentor Books, 1960.

STEVENS, S. S. Psychology and the Science of Science. *Psychological Bulletin,* 1939, *36,* 221–263.

THORNDIKE, E. L. *Psychology of Wants, Interests, and Attitudes.* New York: Appleton-Century, 1935.

TITCHENER, E. B. *Lectures on the Experimental Psychology of the Thought-Processes.* New York: Macmillan, 1909.

TITCHENER, E. B. Description *vs.* Statement of Meaning. *American Journal of Psychology,* 1912, *23,* 165–182.

TITCHENER, E. B. Brentano and Wundt: Empirical and Experimental Psychology. *American Journal of Psychology,* 1921, *32,* 108–120.

TOLMAN, E. C. Theories of Learning. In F. A. Moss (Ed.), *Comparative Psychology.* New York: Prentice-Hall, 1934.

TOLMAN, E. C. The Determiners of Behavior at a Choice Point. *Psychological Review,* 1938, *45,* 1–41.

TOMKINS, S. *The Psychology of Knowledge.* Unpublished manuscript. Invited address, Division 8, American Psychological Association, 1964.

TUKEY, J. W. The Future of Data Analysis. *Annals of Mathematical Statistics,* 1962, *33,* 1–67.

UNDERWOOD, B. J., DUNCAN, C. P., TAYLOR, J. A., and COTTON, J. W. *Elementary Statistics.* New York: Appleton-Century-Crofts, 1954.

USPENSKY, J. V. *Introduction to Mathematical Probability.* New York: McGraw-Hill, 1937.

WAITZ, T. *Introduction to Anthropology.* London: Longman, Green, Longman, and Roberts, 1863.

WALD, A. Contributions to the Theory of Statistical Estimation and

Testing Hypotheses. *Annals of Mathematical Statistics,* 1939, *10,* 299–326.

WALD, A. *Statistical Decision Functions.* New York: Wiley, 1950.

WALD, A. *Selected Papers in Statistics and Probability.* New York: McGraw-Hill, 1955.

WASHBURN, M. F. Introspection as an Objective Method. *Psychological Review,* 1922, *29,* 89–112.

WATSON, J. B. Psychology as the Behaviorist Views It. *Psychological Review,* 1913, *20,* 158–177.

WEBER, M. *The Protestant Ethic and the Spirit of Capitalism.* Translated by Talcott Parsons. New York: Scribner, 1958.

WILSON, K. V. Subjectivist Statistics for the Current Crisis. *Contemporary Psychology,* 1961, *6,* 229–231.

Acknowledgments

I wish to make the following acknowledgments for permission to use my copyrighted materials: The *American Journal of Psychology* for "The Exponential Growth Function in Herbart and Hull," 1952, *65,* 307–308; The American Psychological Association for "The Test of Significance in Psychological Research," in *Psychological Bulletin,* 1966, *66,* 423–437; "A Generalization of Sidman's Results on Group and Individual Functions," in *Psychological Bulletin,* 1954, *51,* 63–64; "A Reconsideration of the Problem of In-

179

trospection," in *Psychological Bulletin,* 1954, *51,* 105–118; "Learning and the Scientific Enterprise," in *Psychological Review,* 1953, *60,* 45–59; "Learning and the Principle of Inverse Probability," in *Psychological Review,* 1953, *60,* 360–370; "The Mystery-Mastery Complex in Contemporary Psychology," in *American Psychologist,* 1965, *20,* 186–191; "Clinical Psychology and Logic," in *American Psychologist,* 1956, *11,* 655–662; the *Catholic Psychological Record* for "Science, Mysticism, and Psychoanalysis," 1966, *4,* 1–9, and "Psychological Characteristics of Man Projected in the Image of Satan," 1967, *5,* 8–15; the *Christian Scholar* for "Idolatry in Religion and Science," 1961, *44,* 223–230; the *Journal of Existential Psychiatry* for "Suicide and the Method of Introspection," 1962, *2,* 313–322; the *Merrill-Palmer Quarterly of Behavior and Development* for "Psychotherapist: Healer or Repairman," 1962, *8,* 129–132; *Perceptual and Motor Skills* for "The General and the Aggregate: A Methodological Distinction," 1955, *5,* 211–212; and *Social Science* for "A Perspective on Psychoanalytic Theory," 1965, *40,* 195–202.

Index

R